Cover Design: Jonathan Truong

Cover Photography: Danya Ensing

Layout & Typography Design: Taylor Chung

Featuring: Tian Shi, Jennifer Ngo, Jonathan Kim, D'Tanga Small

Ryerson
Entrepreneur
Institute

Published 2012 by the Ryerson Entrepreneurship Institute

www.ryerson.ca/rei

REI was created in 2008 to leverage the efforts of our award-winning Students in Free Enterprise (SIFE) team, and the Entrepreneurship and Strategy Department of the Ted Rogers School of Management to make innovation and entrepreneurship support more accessible to all students and alumni from the university across diverse faculties.

REI is a university-wide program, initiated by the Office of the Provost, to motivate students and alumni to actively discover new for-profit and non-profit innovations and act on them to start up new businesses, non-profit organizations or community programs.

This is the first in a series of Entrepreneurial Field Manuals from the Department of Entrepreneurship & Strategy at the Ted Rogers School of Management at Ryerson University. This book was made possible by:

Find out more at: *www.ryerson.ca/ent*

To My mysa,
finder of all things lost,
most of all My heart.

FOREWORD:

The Cold, Hard, Truth by Kevin O'Leary[1]

For more than two decades, not a day has gone by without a pitch. In airports, in limos, in tea houses, even in an outhouse, total strangers come up to me and pitch what they promise is "going to be the best thing I ever saw!" So for more than two decades, not a day has gone by without me having to tell some hard working entrepreneur that their idea sucks.

The truth is that truly great ideas, ideas that lead to creative destruction and change the world forever, are few and far between. Over the last five years, I've probably heard more than 10,000 pitches (through O'Leary Funds, Shark Tank and Dragons' Den). That is a lot of pitches folks. And truth be told, most of them sucked. Yes, there have been some nice investments. But how many were truly disruptive ideas? How many were truly game changing opportunities? How many were ventures that led to huge returns? Few. Great opportunities are few and far between.

It pains me to see good entrepreneurs chase bad opportunities. After all, time, energy, bandwidth and, most of all, M-O-N-E-Y, are all scarce resources. Today, there simply isn't enough time, money, or energy to pursue every idea. And that is a good thing. It leads to evolutionary economics, where only the most agile survive and only the best thrive. It is because of this scarcity, (scarcity in both great opportunities and limited resources) one has to be extremely careful of where one invests. That is true no matter what you invest: money, time, or energy. It doesn't matter if you are an investor backing a Startup with seed capital or an R&D manager deciding

---

[1]Kevin O'Leary currently anchors three televisions show on business and finance: ABC's SHARK TANK; CBC's DRAGONS' DEN and the Lang & O'Leary Exchange. He is the author of the bestselling Cold Hard Truth and Chair of the O'Leary Funds. www.KevinOleary.com

where to allocate limited resources to maximize innovation. You have to be picky.

As the Merchant of Truth, it is my duty to help hard working people put down their rabid dog of an idea and move on. It is my duty to hold them accountable to themselves. It is my duty to help them see the folly of their ways.

Why? Because it pains me to see talented people wilfully blind themselves to the flaws apparent to all. It hurts me to watch a family go bankrupt because their business dreams have become an entrepreneurial nightmare. It hurts me to see scarce resources like seed capital squandered. For all those reasons, and so many more, I help people find the winners and run away from the losers.

So how do you know which opportunities to back and which opportunities to whack? How can you pick the ideas to go all in on? You can find some of these answers in the pages that follow. This book is a concise and accurate tool for opportunity evaluation. It will explain how to separate the best from the rest. If you love DRAGONS' DEN and SHARK TANK, you will love this book. The advice within will save you time, money and most of all, heartbreak.

Table of Contents

A Few words from the Author

Over the last ten years I have spent the majority of my time evaluating entrepreneurial opportunities. First as Director of Ernst & Young's Venture Capital Advisory Group, then as a venture capitalist for a New York-based private equity firm and most recently as the Industry Advisory for the hit business reality show, Dragons' Den (aka Shark Tank). I've chaired the national venture conferences, judged dozens of business plan competitions, and I have worked with over 15,000 entrepreneurs.

In total, I estimate that I've heard more than 10,000 pitches. As a result, I have become very good at picking apart presentations, not based on their delivery but on their flawed content. But there are only so many hours in the day and for every pitch I am able to coach, there are dozens that get lost in the process. I wrote this book hoping to share the tools I've created with others.

Perhaps after using these tools investors will make better funding decisions. Perhaps after reading this, entrepreneurs will be better equipped to shape their ideas into opportunities. Perhaps after reading this you will have a better understanding of why some opportunities fail while others fly.

No matter who you are (entrepreneur, student or investor) I'm hoping that you will enjoy reading this text and I hope even more that it will help you make better decisions about where to invest your precious, scarce resources (your time, your money, your mental bandwidth).

I'm always looking to upgrade this text with more examples. If you have an example that you feel would be of value to include, please email me directly. Should you have any questions, concerns or suggestions, please feel free to contact me directly: sean.wise@ryerson.ca

Onwards and Upwards!

Professor Sean Wise
Professor of Entrepreneurship & Strategy

Part I: Introduction

The Process and Purpose of Opportunity Evaluation

It All Starts With the Idea

There is that magical moment in every entrepreneur's life when a flash of clarity and an amazing idea of how to solve one of our many worldly problems pops into his or her head. Entrepreneurs often have an interesting story to tell about this moment. But before you jump off the couch and invest time and money into your venture, every entrepreneur must ask, "Is there enough demand for this product that people will people will pay for it?"

To answer this question, there are many factors that need to be examined and the factors presented here will give some direction as to how this question may be answered.

Consider the compelling unmet need: Does your product fulfill someone's need? How compelled is the customer to fulfill this need? Is your product something they cannot live without, or is it just a nice-to-have? Is it medication you need to lower blood pressure or is it a cough candy for your sore throat? The greater the pain your product solves, the greater the demand for it. The greater the pain your product solves, the more you can charge for it.

Consider the case of the Startup product Gelfast[2], a hygiene dispenser that can be clipped to a doctor's waist, allowing the doctor to wash his or her hands between tending to each patient. Therefore, Gelfast significantly reduces the rate of hospital acquired infections. Without Gelfast, doctors would not wash their hands as frequently as hygiene dispensers are typically placed in a fixed location, such as down the hall from the examining rooms. Gelfast is a great product idea and it has managed to gain interest from the Dragons because the pain it solves is so great. Research shows that in the United States, hospital acquired infections lead to over 2 million illnesses, 26,000 deaths and an added expenditure of over $4.5 billion each year. This information helps the seller identify who the potential customers might be.

---

[2]www.medonyx.com

In Gelfast's case it is not the doctors, but rather it is the hospital administrators. As a hospital administrator, saving lives and money would be very compelling reasons to buy Gelfast products.

It is not good enough that you think it's a good idea, others need to agree with you to such a degree that they'd be willing to pay for it. When a great idea comes to you, ask others if it is something they'd be willing to pay for, and if possible, ask experts in the related industry for their opinions. Of course, many entrepreneurs are afraid to share their idea with others for fear that it might be stolen from them. To mitigate this risk, speak to only those who are inside your network and those you can trust. Not only can these people inform you on the quality of the idea but they can also help you improve on the idea.

If it's a good idea, chances are someone else is already doing it, so the first thing you should do is perform an Internet search on the idea to see if there is any existing competition or if there are already potential substitutes. If you find anything similar, you must take these competitors seriously. If you don't, you may find yourself in an unfortunate situation, just like the idea pitcher from ePawn World. He wanted to take pawn shops online where people could buy and sell items they would normally bring to a pawn shop, but he did not take eBay or Craigslist seriously as competitors who have already addressed this need.

Below are some ways to find an un-served need:

- Identify an irritation. Take traffic for example—if you could find a way to significantly reduce traffic, many governments would be willing to pay plenty of money for your idea.
- Overcome an assumption, such as "garbage has no use or value". For example, find a use for sleeves that have been taken off garments. Recycling companies take other people's trash for cheap and turn them into someone else's treasure— they sell junk at a profit.

- React to jealousy. WestJet and Porter airlines strive to provide better customer service than the competition and it works— both airlines have developed loyal customers.
- Changes in technology. With the introduction of the Internet, Amazon.com was able to build one of the world's largest bookstores without ever opening a "real" bookstore.

When that brilliant idea pops in your head, remember it is only worth investing your precious time and effort to turn the idea into a real business if people are willing to pay their hard earned money for it.

What is an opportunity?

At some time in your life you've had an entrepreneurial epiphany. Suddenly your brain came up with an idea that could make your rich. An idea that could change the world. An idea that could be your opportunity for fame and fortune.

If you are Mark Zuckerberg that idea might have been Facebook. If you are Elon Musk it might have been PayPal, or Tesla Motors or even SpaceX.
In the annals of time, whenever there is problem or an unmet need, people will try to fix it. These unmet needs are referred to in academia as **sub optimal solutions**.

The telegraph was invented to address the fact that the postal service was a sub optimal solution for rapid communication. Airplanes fixed the suboptimal solution to long voyages by ship. Facebook shifts the **utility curve** when it comes sharing information amongst your friends and family.

But why are some ideas seen as opportunities while others are seen as delusions? What makes an idea an opportunity?

Four Criteria of an Opportunity

All opportunities start with an idea. And while ideas are at the heart of all opportunities[3], for an idea to be seen as an opportunity, the following four axioms[4] must be true:

> 1) The idea is **durable**: The idea is not a fad and will last long enough to allow for monetization.
> 2) The idea is **timely**: The market is ready to buy the solution this idea encompasses.

---

[3]J.A. Timmons. (1994). New Venture Creation: Entrepreneurship for the 21st Century, 4th Edition, Burr Ridge, IL: Irwin.
[4]J.A. Timmons. (1994). "Opportunity Recognition: The Search for Higher Potential Ventures," in Bygrave, W.D (ed.), The Portable MBA in Entrepreneurship, 26-54, Toronto: John Wiley & Sons.

3) The idea is **attractive**: The potential rewards and returns on investment far exceed the foreseeable costs and resources.
4) The idea **adds value**: The idea must lead to a product or service which creates or adds value for its buyer or end user.

Where do opportunities come from?

This book is about opportunity evaluation not opportunity creation and it is beyond the scope of this text to fully explore such. Notwithstanding, the topic should be addressed briefly.

Any time a large population's needs are unsatisfied, entrepreneurs see opportunity. Whenever new technology opens up new solutions, there is opportunity. Every demographic shift leads to opportunity. If new discoveries lead to new possibilities, then they also lead to opportunity.

At the heart of every opportunity lies an unmet need. In fact, the larger the need (either by intensity or population) the quicker the adoption.

What is opportunity evaluation?

Sometimes one simply knows by intuition that a product or service is bound for greatness. It doesn't take a genius to know that the human desire for sex would lead to huge sales of Viagra®. Likewise, one can see the value of email in an ever shrinking globe. However, unlike Viagra® and email, most opportunities are harder to quantify—either because the market for such solutions is unknown or because the idea is so radical.

Since our time, energy, bandwidth and capital are scarce, we have to be able to differentiate the good opportunities from the bad ideas. This is true no matter what role you play in the entrepreneurial ecosystem:

- Entrepreneurs have to choose which opportunity to pursue.
- Investors have to choose which opportunities to fund.
- Government and NGOs need to decide which opportunities are worthy of public resources.
- R&D managers have to decide which innovations to explore.

Thus, opportunity evaluation is generally defined as the systematic objective assessment of a venture's potential. Please note that the quantum of return (i.e., how much money you can make) is not the only driving measure in opportunity evaluation. Investors refer to the quantum of return as ROI, which stands for **Return on Investment** and represents how much money (and other benefits) will be generated by the investment. For example,

The ROI of a one year 3% government bond, is 3%. If you bought $1000 of bonds, you would receive $1030 at the end of the year (your original investment plus 3%, or $30). Besides ROI there is also the probability of success to take into account. After all, a billion dollar idea that fails isn't as good as a million dollar idea that succeeds.

Who is this book for?

This book is for entrepreneurs trying to decide which idea to take to market. This book is for business managers deciding which internal projects to back. This book is for students watching Dragons' Den or Shark Tank who want to better understand the judges' perspectives. This book is for investors looking for a systematic and objective review of funding opportunities. If you have ever had to look at two opportunities and decide which one is more likely to succeed, this book is for you.

Why measure at all?

Considering the degree of unknown factors (for example, uncertain market, unproven demand and technical feasibility) involved in opportunity evaluation, many students ask why measure at all? After all, if most of the inputs are best guesses on future states (e.g., what is the pro forma revenue projection for year 3?) how reliable can the output be?

While the foregoing is true (most information used in opportunity evaluation is estimated at best); it is equally true for all opportunities. As a result, while not objectively valid (i.e., a high score does not guarantee a high chance for success) the opportunity evaluation process is internally valid. This allows us to compare two radically different ideas (both enmeshed by uncertainty) with some confidence. Or put another way, a high score doesn't guarantee a chance of success; it only predicts that opportunities with high scores should outperform opportunities with low scores. To make matters worse, there is no post facto way of confirming this as ideas that score low aren't pursued, making it impossible to know if they would have succeeded.

Notwithstanding, this book is meant to provide readers with a framework formally unknown to the general population. It is designed to ensure that entrepreneurial enthusiasm isn't driving your decisions on which ventures to pursue.

Where does Opportunity Evaluation fit into the overall entrepreneurship process?

Most attempts to model the entrepreneurial process (including the famous Timmons Model[5]) note opportunity evaluation as a key stage in the formulization of a new venture. Typically, it is advisable to look before you leap, and evaluating an opportunity before investing time and energy (and money!) is the best way to do that. Below are two diagrams taken from the academic literature that showcase the role of opportunity evaluation in the entrepreneurship process.

Model 1: From "Formalizing the front-end of the entrepreneurial process using the stage-gate model as a guide[6]," by Barringer and Gresock (2008) we see opportunity evaluation in stages 2 and 3 below.

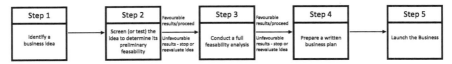

Model 2: From Bolton & Thomson (2004), note Stage 3.

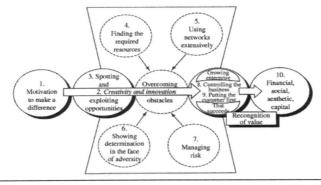

---

[5]J.A. Timmons and S. Spinelli. (2003). New venture creation, entrepreneurship for the 21st century, 6th ed. Toronto: McGraw-Hill.
[6]Bruce B. Barringer & Amy R. Gresock. (2008). "Formalizing the front-end of the entrepreneurial process to improve entrepreneurship education and practice." Journal of Small Business and Enterprise Development, 15(2): 289-303.

What is the cost of poor Opportunity Evaluation?

According to the Global Entrepreneurship Monitor[7] in 2010,

> "Some 110 million people between 18–64 years old were actively engaged in starting a business. Another 140 million were running new businesses they started less than 3½ years earlier. Taken together, some 250 million were involved in early-stage entrepreneurial activity."

But how many were pursuing poor opportunities? How much time, effort and money were tied up in bad ideas? How much do poor opportunity evaluation cost us all?

There are opportunities around us each day. Some are good and some are not. Most people fixate on the "opportunities missed." In over a decade of venture capital, I have heard statements like the following dozens of times: *"XYZ is a great business. I had the idea for XYZ years earlier."*

The statement's speaker will then go on to opine on how wealthy they would be if they had pursued the idea for XYZ. The problem of course is that success is measured post facto (after the fact). So the inventor first sees that XYZ can succeed before seeing how much money it could generate. This retroactively endorses the idea without forcing the entrepreneur to act upon it. Put another way, Mark Zuckerberg was not the first to explore Social Networks; but now that it is a huge success, many people want to take credit for it.

But even the cost of "what could have been" is infinitesimally small when compared to the resources squandered on bad ideas and the costs associated with them.

If Mr. G spends all his time, energy, social capital, bandwidth and money on idea Z. And if idea Z turns out to be a poor opportunity;

---

[7] www.gemconsortium.org

© Sean Evan Wise

then Mr. G is not only out all the time, energy, social capital bandwidth and money he invested in idea Z but he also has an additional **Opportunity Cost**.

According to Investorpedia.com[8], Opportunity Cost represents:

1. The cost of an alternative that must be forgone in order to pursue a certain action.
2. The benefits you could have received by taking an alternative action.

For example, if an executive decides to go back to school to obtain his MBA. here will be direct costs (tuition, school books, bus fare, etc.) and there will be opportunity costs (salary not earned while in school; work promotions not pursuing, etc.). In order to understand the true cost of the MBA, one has to account for both direct costs and opportunity costs.

Take Farmer Q for example. Farmer Q owns 100 acres of prime agricultural land. Farmer Q has a choice; she can grow Carrots or Potatoes (or some mixture). But if she grows carrots which later go out of fashion (or there is a large oversupply of carrots produced) driving the price of carrots down before she can sell her crop; then not only will Famer Q loose the money invested in the carrots and not only will she loose the revenue that those carrots would have generated; but she also loses the money she could have made in potatoes.

So what does poor opportunity evaluation cost us? Well, there is the capital, energy, attention and passion that is wasted, but there is also the opportunity cost. For every bad idea that moves forward lowers the resources available for the better ones.

Venture capitalists invested $21.8 billion in 3,277 deals in 2010[9]. In the venture capital industry it is widely accepted that on average, that only 1 in 100 pitches to a VC get funded. Based on this rule, we

---

[8]www.investopedia.com/terms/o/opportunitycost.asp
[9]www.NVCA.com

can see that if 3,200+ deals got funded, then at least 300,000+ pitches did not get funding that year. Yet, of the 1000+ entrepreneurs who pitched me personally in 2010, each enthusiastically proclaimed their idea was the "best I would ever see!" So why the disconnect? In three words: Poor Opportunity Evaluation.

In 2011, 61% of non-business owners say they want to start a business[10]. Yet on average less than half of these ideas will service 5 years. A third of them will be dead within 24 months. If only entrepreneurs and inventors spent more time evaluating opportunities and less time pitching them.

In the last decade I've heard over 10,000 pitches. Not one of them thought there idea was weak. Tune into Shark Tank® or Dragons' Den® any week and for every great idea you see, you will sell half a dozen not so great ones. Yet before they enter the Tank (or Den) each whole heartedly believes there idea is the best. If only they weren't so weak in opportunity evaluation they would save themselves so much heartache, wasted time and lost capital.

---

[10]www.sba.gov

Page 30 Hot or Not?   © Sean Evan Wise

How to use this book

This book is meant to provide the reader with a formal, objective tool to evaluation opportunities. Narcissistically, I've named this tool the WiseGuide™ and you can see it in action online at:

www.USEtheWiseGuide.com

Following this introductory section, we will move directly into defining and demonstrating how to score the 44 elements that make up the WiseGuide™ scoring system.

In Part III we discuss potential pitfalls that can kill a great venture. Even though we leave this discussion until after the 44 elements are illustrated, in the "real world" opportunity evaluators typically check for pitfalls first, and only upon finding none do they undertake a more thorough review. Because of this, the framework presented here follows a Stage-Gate model[11] of decision making.

Part III is followed by a "Tool Kit" of the concepts in action. This section is meant to illustrate how the elements come into play as well as provide the reader with practical and grounded examples from the real world.
For the most part, examples come from my work as a venture capitalist and from my years of experience working with the business reality show, Dragons' Den (also known as Shark Tank).

We have also been blessed to have contributions from leaders in opportunity evaluation. We have spread these short essays throughout the text in the hope that their perspectives will help round out readers' opinions. These sections will be easy to spot, as the author's name is listed below the subsection.

Finally, knowing the issues with your opportunity is only the start of the process of opportunity assessment. Smart evaluators also

---

[11]en.wikipedia.org/wiki/Stage–gate_model

look to see which elements could be quickly, easily and successfully upgraded and evolved. Sometimes, an investor brings domain. To help with this evolution process we have added, wherever applicable, a section entitled Raising the Score.

How to gather the data needed

This text is not a guide to Due Diligence. It is not meant to cover all the variables that need to be accounted for prior to commitment. It is simply a starting point for opportunity evaluation. It is meant to facilitate an exploratory conversation and to help opportunity evaluators decide if more attention is warranted. As a result, external references are not required. Third party evidence is required. Why?

All entrepreneurs think they have the next great thing, as a result investors and other opportunity evaluators can't rely on self-serving statements. Instead, whenever possible, seek out third party, arms' length information. What are your actual sales? What have your potential clients said? Who else believes in the greatness of your opportunity?

Quality of Evidence

The stronger the evidence presented, the higher the score. The greater your ability to prove your assumptions using external validation, the better the score. For example, sales are great but sales to well-known brands are even better. Saying that your product is needed is good but showing the rapid adoption of the product is better.

To account for this in your assessment, give extra points for any element that is presented with third party evidence (footnotes, sales receipts, feedback from focus groups).

The Credibility Factor

When you Google your name, what hits do you see? Perhaps that paper you wrote in university, maybe your LinkedIn profile, or possibly pictures from that conference you attended. Do they portray you in a positive light?

In any partnership "trust" is essential, and every investor wants to ensure you're truthful because, ultimately, they need to trust you with their money. In the beginning, every investor will check over two things:

1. Are the entrepreneur's claims true?
2. The reputation of the entrepreneur

It's difficult enough to build a business from scratch, imagine doing that with a partner you can't trust. With this in mind, entrepreneurs must be completely honest with investors and only make claims they can back up. Too often entrepreneurs turn into blowfish before meet their investors. These are the entrepreneurs who to "inflate" themselves moments before the presentation and over valuate their companies, and the inflation always shows through.

Upholding the highest level of honesty and integrity and making claims that you can back up ensures investors will perceive you as credible. This credibility earns trust, convincing investors you will use their money wisely.

How to use the WiseGuide™

At the back of this book and online at www.USEtheWiseGuide.com, you will find a template worksheet for opportunity evaluation. It has been broken down into eight categories and each category is weighted. The weighting is based on feedback from more than 100 professional investors.

The eight categories cover the major areas reviewed in the opportunity evaluation process are listed below:

- **P**eople ⇨ who is behind the project?
- **P**ain ⇨ what problem are you addressing?

- **P**roduct ⇨ what solution do you offer?
- **P**rovince ⇨ to what market or industry are you selling?
- **P**itch ⇨ how will you deliver a clear, two-minute overview?
- **P**lan ⇨ what is your go-to-market strategy?
- **P**roposal ⇨ what are you seeking to gain, what are you willing to give?
- **P**itfalls ⇨ what things should you avoid?

In each of these eight categories, there are several sub-elements. Each will be rated by the reviewer. Ratings go from -10 (very bad) to +10 (very good). In total there are 44 elements in the WiseGuide™. Each element has a rating and that rating is multiplied based on the importance and impact (5 for impactful, 3 for important, 1 for average). The weighting is based on investor experience.

Weightings are based on the impact that each element may have on an investment decision and may relate to investor capital, investor time and so on. To represent these relative weights, I have assigned a multiplier to each element based on categories:

- **P**eople ⇨ 5x
- **P**ain ⇨ 5x
- **P**roduct ⇨ 3x
- **P**rovince ⇨ 3x
- **P**itch ⇨ 1x
- **P**lan ⇨ 1x
- **P**roposal ⇨ 1x

The result should be a number between -1340 and 1340.

What is a good score?

"Good" is a very subjective term. The top score possible on the WiseGuide™ is 1340. For those who are extremely risk adverse you would want your score to be no less than 1150 (85%). For those who are more entrepreneurial in nature, no less than 810 (60%) or more makes the opportunity worth pursuing.

However, I would caution against this type of thinking. Instead, look for the opportunity in which you have a competitive advantage. If you have deeper Domain Knowledge in opportunity 1 than opportunity 2, it might be worth pursuing opportunity 1 even if it has a lower overall WiseGuide™ score.

On a similar note, once you have generated an opportunity's WiseGuide™, revisit the lower scoring elements. Consider if you are able to impact that score. Perhaps you find a partner with Business Acumen, taking that key element from a -5 to a +10. Perhaps you might be able to secure some IP, raising that element from a 0 to a +5. In other words, don't simply calculate the score and walk away. Examine the scorecard with your partners and determine if any elements could be improved.

---

[12]Based on a survey of 500+ innovation investors.

© Sean Evan Wise

Hot or Not? **Page 35**

Same Opportunity, Different Scores

Two investors are unlikely to generate the same score, even for the same opportunity pitched at the same time. The main reason for this is that each reviewer has their own experiences that impact their reception of the pitch. These differing experiences influence how they perceive risk and in turn how they rate each element. As a result, two reviewers may see the same facts, but perceive them differently. Don't be disturbed by this. The key is not to have an absolute score but a relative. Is opportunity A better than opportunity B? Is B better than C? Once again, this leads to internal validity (I use the same experiences to judge each opportunity) but scores will be different from reviewer to reviewer. This raises the issue of bias.

© Sean Evan Wise

The Issue of Bias

Opportunity evaluation is a highly subjective process. Each reviewer will not only base a venture's score on the information presented by the founder, but each score will also be impacted by the reviewer's personal history, experience and bias. This last item is of most concern. Biases can impact scores greatly, often creating a blind spot that can be difficult to mitigate. It is thus important to first assess oneself before assessing others.

Killer bias: Psychological traps that catch entrepreneurs and investors

By Professor Dave Valliere, MEng MBA PhD PEng

There are all kinds of people who need to know how to spot a great business idea. Some are entrepreneurs trying to decide whether this is the opportunity they should put their heart and soul into. Some are investors trying to discover the one that will yield returns big enough to offset all the other dog investments they've made. Some are potential employees, suppliers, business partners, or intermediaries. Each has a different perspective and different objective for the opportunity evaluation process. But all operate with the same flawed human mind, trying to assess the idea and potentially falling prey to the same common psychological biases—the kinds of traps that catch everyone unless we are fully aware of them and take steps to avoid them. The following are four of the most pervasive psychological biases that often trick both entrepreneurs and their investors into making bad decisions. Decisions that can kill new ventures and wipe out investments.

Confirmation bias or, as it is sometimes known, **wilful blindness** arises whenever we have formed a strongly held opinion or view about something, particularly when we have made a big effort to gather and analyze a lot of information before arriving at our opinion

---

[11]en.wikipedia.org/wiki/Stage–gate_model

(exactly like when developing a business plan). There are two dangerous effects that may result from confirmation bias. The first is that reviewers become very attuned and receptive to information that appears to support their opinions. For instance, they tend to notice every newspaper article that can be interpreted to support their belief. Reviewers who have fallen prey to confirmation bias tend to view and accept as true every occurrence in the world that can possibly be seen as an example of the phenomenon in which they believe.

The second dangerous effect of confirmation bias is that reviewers can become quite blind to information that appears to refute their opinion. Reviewers suffering from confirmation bias often cease to look for information that might contradict their preformed opinion (why bother, since they "know" their opinions must be right). Furthermore, if the world shoves the conflicting information into their faces they find some way to rationalize it or deny it (they say "yeah, but...," and then find some trivial difference that allows them to dismiss the contradictory evidence as an irrelevant "special case") rather than change their opinions (since that would mean admitting we were wrong in the first place). It can suddenly seem like confirming cases and examples are everywhere around us and it can seem like no counterevidence exists. But this is an illusion – the rates of occurrence and non-occurrence have not changed. It is only our awareness and perception that has changed.

Because of this, entrepreneurs and other opportunity evaluators should always attempt to remain flexible and open to the possibility that their opinions and assumption may turn out to be false. Opportunity evaluators should attempt to always remain humble and receptive in the face of the reality that the marketplace will try to teach them. They should make sure their assumptions are open to being proved wrong.

But that's often not enough, if these entrepreneurs don't also take active measures to counteract confirmation bias. And, of course, investors face the same risks too (and are generally more difficult to coach), once they've formed an opinion about whether a market space is "hot" or not. Both groups need to take deliberate actions to keep confirmation bias in check, such as deliberately seeking out contradictory information or contrarian opinions from experts. The real test of whether you have a good business idea is not your ability to find information that says "yes," but your inability to find information that says "no".

TIP: To avoid confirmation bias, spend your time trying to find information that refutes your beliefs instead of more information that supports them.

The next killer bias is **over-confidence**, which is having a belief in one's abilities that is greater than the objective facts warrant. While it is good to have entrepreneurs who are highly talented and who know it (confidence), entrepreneurs who are unable to recognize the limits of their remarkable talent (over-confidence) can cause real problems. But this is a particularly hard bias to detect in oneself, since people who are over-confident in their abilities are usually also over-confident in their self-awareness and ability to correct for their own biases. Over-confidence is actually an umbrella term that encompasses a group of related biases, including the **planning fallacy** or "90/90 rule" (i.e., the first 90% of a project takes first 90% of the budget, and the final 10% of the project takes the second 90% of the budget), and **personal attribution error** (i.e., if things go right it's because I'm so smart and skilled, but if things go wrong it's because someone else screwed up). All are examples of having unreasonably high beliefs in oneself.

Psychometric tests of opportunity evaluators like entrepreneurs and investors repeatedly show some amazingly high levels of over-confidence. This is a real cause for worry. These individuals are highly confident and are perfectly right to feel that way since they are highly skilled and able. In fact, one might argue that confidence is a necessary trait for both entrepreneurs and investors. But, while their abilities might well be 50% better than the average person, they tend to think and act as if their abilities were 500% better.

For entrepreneurs, this means they often think they can accomplish much more than they can, and that their chances of succeeding in a risky venture are much better than they are actually. The same phenomenon holds for investors, who will be over-confident in their abilities to pick winners and to add value to their investees (i.e., make sure the investee firms become hugely successful). There's a real lesson in the observation that most VC funds have a hit ratio of only 1-in-10 investees becoming successful. But most VC investors are unable to learn from it because they are caught in their own over-confidence.

TIP: To avoid overconfidence bias, make your decisions based on objective data about what you actually have achieved in the past, not what you subjectively think you should be able to do in future.

The third killer bias is **availability bias**, which is the mistaken belief that situations that are easy for an individual to imagine must therefore be very common out in the world (or the converse, that if you've never personally seen a black swan they must not exist). But, while this is seductive reasoning, it is false logic. It can be extremely dangerous to generalize too widely from our own experience. Our own experience is not typical and is not to be blindly trusted (after all, everyone is abnormal is some way—it's perfectly normal). With proper perspective we can see that our own experience, while a deep and vivid source of insight, is still just a dataset with n=1 as the sample size. One data point is hardly enough to use as the foundation for an entire business strategy. Statisticians will remind us that any sample with fewer than thirty responses will fail to meet even the most basic assumptions of statistical inference. So we sometimes try to guard against this bias by reminding ourselves that the plural of "anecdote" is not "data".

Entrepreneurs who are caught by this bias often exhibit "the market is me" behaviours; they believe that if they like the proposed new product, then thousands of other people are going to like it too. This is a weird conclusion if you think it through. After all, we celebrate entrepreneurs for being so unlike other people, for thinking and

© Sean Evan Wise

seeing so differently than others, and for being willing to act where other people would not. They are therefore not very suitable to use as benchmarks for the marketplace.

Entrepreneurship educators may further compound the problem by (correctly) telling prospective entrepreneurs to seek and exploit opportunities in areas that they know well, where they have prior knowledge and experience that gives them asymmetric information and insight. We often encourage our students to leverage their **Domain Knowledge** obtained from prior experience. This is all well and good, but it does increase the potential for getting trapped by availability bias. And of course, the exact same problem occurs on the investor side of the table. In their case it often sounds something like, "I heard that BigFundCo got a 10X exit in the cloud computing space, so I'm going to invest in the next cloud deal that crosses my desk". This bias affects internal opportunity evaluators too. For example, if one big company's R&D produces a huge winner based on crowdsourcing then R&D managers at other big companies tend to jump on ship, pushing to add crowdsourcing to their repertoire regardless of whether it was the actual cause of the initial success.

TIP: To avoid availability bias, keep reminding yourself that your experience is unique and that there is no reason to think that it corresponds to what real market data would say about the average person.

The final killer bias to be wary of is an interesting phenomenon described by **prospect theory**. Prospect theory explains three interrelated biases. First, people give too much emotional weight to small chances, thinking that a 1% chance is much better than no chance at all and that a 99% chance is much worse than a sure thing (the strength of this belief can be witnessed at any lottery ticket kiosk). Secondly, people treat chances of winning something much differently than they treat the chances of avoiding the loss of something (for example, we usually have to offer the chance of winning at least $250 to entice people to accept a chance of losing $100). Thirdly, people judge these wins and losses not in absolute terms, but relative to where they expected to be or where they told other people that they'd be (their reference or anchor point). These biases combine to create a two-sided irrational phenomenon that catches many people. On the one hand, if we are winning (or even if we are losing, but not as badly as we expected to lose) we tend to become overly conservative and reluctant to take sensible or attractive gambles. We try to lock in our wins, thinking that a bird in the hand is worth two in the bush. On the other hand, if we are losing (or even if we are winning, but not as grandly as we told everyone we would) we tend to become reckless risk-takers who throw "Hail Mary" passes in the slim hope that we can catch up to where we "ought" to be. This phenomenon is the mechanism that drives so-called **escalating commitment**, the throwing of good money after bad in the hopes that the original losses can still be somehow salvaged. This is based on the stubborn human refusal to recognize that **sunk costs** are always irrelevant when making a decision in the present moment. For example, an investor who has watched his share price fall in a clearly doomed Startup company will still be strongly biased to participate in any subsequent round of funding in a futile attempt to keep the company alive for a bit longer to avoid having to accept that the first round money is irretrievably lost.

Prospect theory warns opportunity evaluators that they cannot trust their gut instincts when assessing probabilities of success, and that their perceptions will be strongly skewed by recent history. It says that they must ignore the emotional perception that losses sting them more than wins please them, and that they must be particularly careful when publicly announcing targets (or even just privately setting their hearts and expectations on them) lest they become anchor points that will force them into irrational escalating commitments. Investors may love entrepreneurs who set "kick-ass" targets and (blinded by their over-confidence) loudly proclaim that these **BHAGs** will be achieved or exceeded. But such acts come with huge risks of becoming trapped in killer biases that will drive bad decisions and destroy value.

TIP: To avoid escalating commitment biases arising from prospect theory, use objective calculations to determine the expected value of uncertain choices, and be very careful about the public commitments you make.

Every day, everywhere around the world, opportunities are being evaluated and significant resource commitments are being made. Which Startups to fund? Which R&D projects to support? Which founders to back? These are questions with enormous social and economic consequences. Look around and you'll see these killer biases happening everywhere, including in yourself. And, although you are now among the few people aware of them, remember that they will still affect you unless you take concrete and deliberate steps to avoid them. So remember to do the following whenever you are evaluating opportunities:

1. Spend your time trying to find information that refutes your beliefs, instead of more information that supports them.

2. Make your decisions based on objective data about what you actually have achieved in the past, not what you subjectively think you should be able to do in future.

3. Keep reminding yourself that your experience is unique and that there is no reason to think that it corresponds to what real market data would say about the average person.

4. Use objective calculations to determine the expected value of uncertain choices, and be very careful about the public commitments you make.

Why it all means nothing in the end

The axiom "Garbage in, garbage out" comes to mind when I'm asked if the WiseGuide™ method of Opportunity Evaluation is reliable and accurate. Put bluntly, the scores generated by following this text are only as accurate as the information provided by the entrepreneurs. If the information they provide is incorrect or embellished or even slightly biased, the score may be less reliable.

Further, scores obtained are not cross validated. For example, two reviewers may evaluate the exact same opportunity, at the exact same moment, and still end up with different scores. This is a significant subjective element to this process. And while one reviewer might think a company's IP is worth +10 another may not. Notwithstanding, the scores are internally valid, meaning that two opportunities evaluated at the same time by the same person are fully comparable. It is for this reason that the WiseGuide™ is most useful when comparing different opportunities.

No matter how great the opportunity, in the end it is execution not ideas that creates change and generates wealth.

Execution – What Really Matters!

Professor Steven A. Gedeon, PhD, MBA, PEng

Entrepreneurship is that fundamental spark of human initiative that enables us to act and shape the world around us. It is about belief in yourself, your ability to create positive change, and your capacity to inspire others to join you in your great adventure. It is about starting with nothing but your own mind and creating dramatic new values that never previously existed. Entrepreneurship is the most empowering, creative, freedom-loving power in the world.

Entrepreneurship is more than a business discipline. It is a core way of seeing, thinking and acting that is relevant to all disciplines, all faculties, and all people.

Entrepreneurs don't just see the world as it is, they see it as it can or ought to be. And then they make it happen. Yes, entrepreneurs are visionaries, inventors, planners, thinkers, dreamers and opportunity spotters – but none of those matters if they are not also doers.

Entrepreneurship is about creating value. Value must be brought forth into physical existence before it can be exchanged, sold or used to earn a living. Even something as abstract as Intellectual Property must be crystallized into a concrete form such as a written document (patent), creative work of art (copyright), or logo (trademark).

Execution is everything. An idea or a business plan has no value on its own. Investors say that they invest in an A team with a B plan over a B team with an A plan. Why? Because business plans are wrong. Despite all the great analysis and planning, things will go wrong. Sales may take longer, product development may take longer, founders may leave, a competitor may enter the field – or all these may happen at once. You just don't know.

Stability for a new company is like stability on a motorcycle. When the motorcycle is stationary or moving slowly it easily falls over and seems to weigh a ton. It's hard to get it back up again when it falls or to push it when it's not running. But at high speeds, its spinning wheels act as gyroscopes to keep you upright. Barriers that seemed insurmountable when you were pushing the bike up a hill become slight bumps in the road at high speeds.

The faster you act, the more stable your company becomes and the higher your chances of success. Perfectionists make lousy entrepreneurs. Don't waste time on the perfect business plan – it's probably wrong anyway. Don't delay speaking to customers, making sales or launching your product as you wait for the perfect moment. Get out there – now!

Initiative, passion and execution are the only things that you, the entrepreneur, really have under your direct control. With that in mind, here are a few specific "Principles of Entrepreneurial Execution":

- Be an Evangelist—Get out there and talk to everyone who shows interest in your business including potential customers, suppliers, employees, investors, friends and peers. Don't keep your idea a secret. Don't disclose your secret sauce of course, but if your idea or ability to execute is so weak that others can steal it, then let them take it and move on to something that you can execute better than others.

- Be a Skeptic—Don't just talk—listen! Ask the hard questions and don't let people get away with telling you what they think you want to hear. Don't just hear the nice things people say. Go deeper and keep asking questions until you find something they don't like or understand. You need to tell people great things about your company, but don't let that blind you to the possibility that your company is not as great as it could be.

- Be an Examiner—Set, Measure and Track Goals—There are more things in a business to keep track of than any single human being can accomplish without a serious project management mindset. Accordingly, you need to find a way to track the goals that really matter and focus your team on achieving them. You need to find a way to translate long-term goals into daily action items. These goals have been referred to as Key Business Screamers, Key Success Factors, Milestones, and Targets. You need to make sure everyone is "singing from the same songbook" and project management and goal-setting skills are essential for doing this.

- Tie Rewards to Performance—Align everyone in your organization toward these key metrics. Don't just pay people for showing up and looking busy.

- Tie Organizational Structure to Strategy—Figure out what each of your strategic value chain activities is and put an executive in charge of each one so these key activities don't fall between the cracks. Don't just have an organizational structure that gives each founder a VP title with no corresponding key activity. There is no need to use traditional titles like VP Tech or VP Marketing simply due to a lack of imagination.

- Question your Assumptions and Adapt—Most successful companies make several major course corrections early in their corporate lives. The chances of your business plan being correct are very low—which means that you should assume from the beginning that you will make major changes to your product, team, and target market. Learning entrepreneurs are successful entrepreneurs. As you get out there and present your products and services to your market, you should be learning and changing. If not, you are probably staying a blind course and are destined to fail.

- Be a Role Model—You, the entrepreneur, breathe life into the company you create. Along with this breath of life, you also instil into the company your values, passion, and work ethic. The company culture is the culture that you create through your habits and character. If you show up late, so will your employees. If you can't make and keep commitments, neither will your company. In the early stages of a company, you are the living personification of the character that your company will become. Be a great person in order to lead a great company.

How to practice evaluating opportunities

Never before have so many people been so interested in entrepreneurship. Today, entrepreneurs are the rock stars of the 21st century economy. Opportunity Evaluation is an experientially based skill that requires repetition and use in order to be fully understood.

Each week on millions of television sets around the world, there is a television show which broadcasts the ups, the downs and the passion involved in entrepreneurial innovation. In the USA the show is called Shark Tank. In the Czech Republic it is called Den D. In Afghanistan, it is called Fikr wa Talash. In several Arab countries, Al Aareen. In Israel, Hakrishim. But In Canada, the UK, Finland and in more than a dozen other countries it is called Dragons' Den. No matter what it is called, millions around the world have followed the call of entrepreneurship as a result of watching the show.

I spent five years as the Industry Advisor and Online Host for Dragons' Den. Through the show, I had the chance to evaluate thousands of entrepreneurial opportunities. I have seen the best. I have seen the worst. It is from these experiences along with decade of venture capital that I have based this text.

Each week the hour long show features Startup entrepreneurs seeking investment from financially successful judges. Each week the highs and lows of entrepreneurship are featured as the all-star business panel judges each opportunity, screening for the best. Most of the shows are now available online. By watching even a few hours of pitches, even the most novice opportunity evaluator will find themselves applying the very theories and criteria outlined in this book to judge the merits of each. So tune in, judge along and learn just what it takes for an idea to go from concept to capital.

A few words about Risk, Uncertainty & Ambiguity

There are important but subtle differences between risk, uncertainty and ambiguity. Risk occurs when actions (or inaction) may lead to loss. Risk deals with a future state that may be negative. Risk is perceived as being quantifiable. In contrast, deals with future states that cannot be known and cannot be predicted nor quantified. Ambiguity relates knowledge which is unclear. Entrepreneurs face risk, uncertainty and ambiguity on a daily basis.

Risks can be mitigated. The risk of commodity prices rising, can be mitigated by buying large quantities of the commodity in advance. Unlike risk, uncertainty can only be addressed in the fullness of time. Ambiguity, unlike uncertainty, can be addressed by through proper and full investigation. With that in mind, let's discuss how investors and opportunity evaluators measure risk.

Many entrepreneurs forget that investors are in the business of saying no. Almost 99% of pitches fail to meet the minimum to attract investor interest. Professional investors (e.g., venture capitalists) are in the business of generating returns from a portfolio approach (e.g., they invest in many, but reap rewards from few). For most investors, analyzing risk is as important as exploring potential returns.

Risk can be classified into three overreaching categories: market risk, magic risk and management risk.

Market Risk asks: If you build it, will they come? If you make a product that addresses a pain point, will the market respond? Market Risk is most easily addressed through sales.

Magic Risk asks: If you build it, will it be 10x better? Can your innovation address market needs in such a way as to lead to creative destruction? Magic Risk is most easily addressed by third party's arm's length comparative report.

Management Risk asks: Is this the best team to back? Do they have a full Talent Triangle in place? Has the team "Been there, done that"? Management's track record helps address management risk.

There is no way to avoid risk. In fact, it is risk that leads to opportunity. As a result of this inalienable fact, those pitching innovations should not only explicitly recognize key risks but outline how those risks will be mitigated. Innovators should focus on those risks specific to their venture or concept and avoid mentioning the risks that all opportunities face. Here are a few risks that ALL new innovations must overcome, opportunity evaluators accept these risks as present always and thus need not be referenced.

For example:

All innovations must attract early adopters, and there is always a risk that this won't happen. Therefore don't include this risk.

Wikipedia faced a risk that consumers of encyclopaedic information were also willing to edit and create such information for the benefit of others. This risk is specific to Wikipedia and therefore should be addressed, perhaps with evidence.

To mitigate risk, many investors seek proof of concept before investing. Before 2000, proof of concept was often defined as: I turn on the light, and the light goes on, thus the technology worked. Today, proof of concept has evolved and many Angels (and Dragons) want to ensure that not only that the light goes on but also that someone will pay to read under the light.

Customers (as proof of concept) speak volumes by purchasing and sales represent not only proof that the market for the product exists but sales help to show that the team behind the Startup is good enough to generate such sales. Sales not only help offset market risk, they offset management risk.

Part II: The 44 WiseGuide™ Elements

Introduction

The following sections detail 44 different criteria (elements) that make up an opportunity evaluation using the WiseGuide™ system.

Elements are grouped into categories (e.g., People, Pain, Product, etc.) and each category is weighted (for example, People is worth more than Plan).

During a pitch, opportunity evaluators should keep track of which elements have been addressed and ask follow up questions about the elements not mentioned.

For each element, the reviewer will first need to decide the relative strength of the item. Strength runs along a continuum:

- -10.......very bad, undermines the opportunity
- -5.........poor, but not the worse it could be
- 0..........not applicable or neutral
- +5........this element benefits the opportunity
- +10......best of the best

The scores should be tracked using the WiseGuide™ template found in Schedule B of Part III of this text. Once all elements are scored and weighted, they should be aggregated and compared to other historical scores the reviewer has previously studied.

People

A decade ago, I ran a survey for the accounting firm Ernst & Young. I asked Startup investors to weigh various elements used in their investment decision process. By far the most important of all the categories is PEOPLE. People elements make up 40% of the overall decision matrix. That is why you often hear investors quote mantras like:

- Bet on the jockey, not the horse.
- An A team with a B idea beats a B team with an A idea.
- PEOPLE is to opportunity, as PLACE is to real estate.

The reasons for this are obvious: people execute. Without people to drive the business, all you have is a good idea. Further reasons for weighing PEOPLE elements disproportionately include the fact that while most elements evolve (markets change, products advance) over time, people are the hardest elements to change and are often the slowest to evolve. While it is true that most investors include Management Controls (e.g., investors can fire the CEO) most investors are averse to changing the business's founders.

The People category can be broken down into a number of elements. These elements may represent both skills sought by investors (e.g., Business Acumen) or attributes historically proven to increase the probability of a venture's success (e.g., Coachable).

Element 1: Working on it Full Time

What is it?

Count the number of people who are working (paid or unpaid) on the opportunity.

Why it matters?

Ideas don't count, execution counts and execution requires focused founders. If no one is working on this opportunity full time, how will it progress? The more people who are working full time (or who are "all in") the more confidence investors will have. After all, if founders won't take the risk and quit their jobs, why would investors take the risk and fund it?

Questions to ask

How many team members work on this venture full time? How long have they been at it? Why aren't more people focused on this full time if it is so great? Why haven't you gone "all in"?

How to score this element:

Score this opportunity a:

- -10 if ...no one is working on the project full time.
- -5 if ...the founders are willing to quit after funding.
- 0 if ...one founder is working full time.
- 5 if ...all founders are working full time for pay.
- 10 if ...all founders working on it full time for free.

Raising the Score

This element is all about commitment. If you aren't able to work on the venture full time, how else might you show commitment? Would a pledge to join the venture full time post funding raise the score? Perhaps, but the more the idea's proponents show real commitment (money, time opportunity cost). To raise this score, show what the idea's champions have sacrificed to bring the opportunity to light.

Element 2: Been There: Done That

What is it?

All opportunities have some similarities (for example, raising capital, filing taxes, hiring staff) and mistakes made in the past often serve to lessen the mistakes made in the future. Note that not all experience is weighted equally. The most valuable experience comes from leading a Startup through a successful exit (for example, the founder's prior Startup was a success) but all experience (including from a failed Startup) counts.

Why it matters?

Many investors say, "I don't want founders learning on my dime." meaning that a serial entrepreneur is always easier to back than a de novo entrepreneur since their experience increases the probability of success. Other reasons why serial entrepreneurs are often seen as better bets include: more realistic projections and timelines; better access to resources including capital; and more seasoned judgement. It may also be a result of better selection (for example, serial entrepreneurs are able pick better opportunities to pursue, as was found in 2010 by a team of researchers at Harvard[14]).

Examples in action

A Startup scoring high on this element will have founders who are serial entrepreneurs, preferably with at least one strong exit to date.

Questions to ask

On your team, how many have been in Startups before? What happened to those ventures? What did your team do before this opportunity?

How to score this element:

The more Startup experience the higher this element will score. Score this opportunity a:

- -10 if ...founders have no prior Startup experience.
- -5 if ...one founder has some minor Startup experience.
- 0 if ...one founder has Startup experience.
- 5 if ...all founders have Startup experience, but none has had a successful exit.
- 10 if ...all founders are serial entrepreneurs with successful exits.

---

[14]P.Gompers, A.Kovner, J.Lerner and D.Scharfstein. (2010). "Performance persistence in entrepreneurship." Journal of Financial Economics, 96(1): 18-32.

© Sean Evan Wise

Element 3: Coachable

What is it?

Entrepreneurs need thick skin and resilient egos. Without both, founders would not be able to endure the ups and downs of Startup life. All Startups need exuberant passion and stoic dedication. After all, anything new (products, software, solutions) is difficult to get to market. Without perseverance and confidence a Startup wouldn't survive its first year. Often all a founder has at 4 a.m. is his or her passion. But too much passion can lead to overconfidence and **Wilful Blindness**.

Take the pitch for Pristine Cart, a product that sanitizes shopping carts. The idea was flawed because the cost of the solution far outweighed the benefit generated to the person paying for such costs (i.e., the grocery store pays but the benefit is to the customers). The entrepreneur simply refused to acknowledge this fact, even after hearing it from several potential customers. The unfortunate part is that the entrepreneur had already invested $120k into the product, and the investors not only refused to invest, instead they spent most of the time trying to convince the entrepreneur to stop pursuing the business.

The ideal founder has enough confidence in her idea to actively seek out criticism and feedback. After all, a solid innovator knows it is through such feedback that one can spot and address early potential points of resistance. Coachability refers to the founder's openness to external review, questioning and advice.

Why it matters?

Investors, particularly Startup investors, consider themselves to be **Smart Money**. As a result they wish to contribute more than just capital to a venture. They wish to add in their mentorship, their network and, most of all, the lessons learned from experience. For these reasons, investors want to back entrepreneurs who listen as much as talk. Further, they want to fund founders who not only listen to them, but also listen to the market.

Startups change. No business idea ends where it started. In fact, many of the most successful new ventures started elsewhere. Take Viagra™ for example.

Originally developed by Pfizer as a heart medication, Viagra™ quickly became a solution for treating erectile dysfunction. Viagra™ has since become one of the bestselling pharmaceutical products in the world (with more than a billion dollars a year in annual sales, this drug became one of the fastest adopted products in history). Now what would have happened if the intrapreneurs at Pfizer hadn't listened to feedback? Might they still be pushing a hard to sell heart medication?

Examples in action

How many team members work on this venture full time? How long have they been at it? Why aren't more people focused on this full time if it is so great? Why haven't you gone "all in"?

A founder who is coachable will demonstrate such almost immediately. All a reviewer must do is ask a contrarian question such as, "I'm concerned about Google, why don't you think they are a threat?" and see how the founders react. If the entrepreneurs lead with..."Google has no idea how to innovate..." it may be a sign that their ego is impacting their judgement.

Here are some other questions I have seen used to test the coachability of a founder:

1. Where do you see yourself in the company in 3 years?
    i. Bad Answer: Leading the company, I'm the only CEO we will ever need.

ii. Good Answer: Wherever the company needs me.
2. Who on your team knows more than you?
i. Bad Answer: No one.
ii. Good Answer: Everyone, I always surround myself with those with skills I lack.
3. Would you rather be rich or famous?
i. Bad Answer: Famous. I deserve it.
ii. Good Answer: Rich, my primary concern is the return on investment that all stakeholders will receive for contributing to our success.

Questions to ask

How do you determine your strategy? With whom, outside the company, do you regularly speak? What role would you ideally want an investor or board member to play?

How to score this element:

Many investors attempt to gauge the coachability of Startup founders. Give founders that resist all input or who think that they know it all a -10. Give founders who are already actively seeking contrary opinions and leverage such for positive change a +10. Assign a 0 if this element never arose during the opportunity review. Score this element with a -5 if the founders acknowledge the need for coaching, but have not yet acquired such. Give this element a +5 if a mentor or coach is involved, but not leveraged fully (for example, having a board of advisors is good, but only if they meet regularly with the founders).

Raising the Score

Having a mentor in place before you pitch is a good way to raise an opportunity's score. Similarly, being able to put together a dedicated advisory board (one you meet with regularly) speaks volumes to your coachability and can thus also help raise the score.

Element 4: Ability to Attract Talent

What is it?

My team once did a survey that showed that more than 60% of an investor's decision to invest was based on management, which begs the question, What do investors look for when it comes to management? Well, every investor is different, one investor might focus on the entrepreneur's passion while another might focus on the founder's experience, and yet another financier might focus on the entrepreneur's weak spots, hoping that alongside their investment the investor might be able to help address that weakness. Notwithstanding, one thing is true for most, if not all, early stage investors—it all comes down to MANAGEMENT, MANGEMENT, MANAGEMENT.

Venture Capitalists often talk about the well rounded management team. Venture capitalists will look at the entire leadership team, not just the person pitching the deal, to evaluate both its skills and experience. Typically, investors look for what is sometimes called the Talent Triangle. The Talent Triangle is a meme that says there are three distinct sets of skills needed for a Startup to succeed: Business Acumen, Domain Knowledge and operational experience.

Like change, another constant for most Startup opportunities is the fact that they are all under-resourced. I've never met a Startup that has all the resources (capital, people, IP) it needed to succeed. Often, Startups raise capital from investors to address the fact that they need to acquire more resources. The ability to attract assets (including Talent) away from other opportunities invests confidence in potential investors. After all, these resources understand the industry better than the investor, if they are willing to commit, perhaps so should the investor.

Basically, you are looking to explore **Opportunity Cost** as an objective piece of **third party validation**. If the founders all sacrificed high paying jobs to join this Startup, investors may want to find out why. Or, more often, it is framed in the negative: if this opportunity was so good, how come no one has quit their job to work on it full time?

Why it matters?

The most important resource is of course human capital. The ability to attract talent to join your Startup is a key skill. If a founder can show success in attracting a new team member by stealing them away from their current position, then investors will gain confidence in the opportunity. Imagine you are able to hire away the VP of Sales from Facebook. Doing so will imply that your opportunity is better than Facebook, and that's something that catches the attention of seasoned investors.

Examples in action

A Startup who has already attracted a high-powered founder away from a seemingly better opportunity will score high on this element.

Questions to ask

How did the staff come together? Did anyone leave a well-paying job to work on this? If the founders weren't hard at work on this venture, what would they be doing?

How to score this element:

Score this element a +10 if the Startup team has already shown an ability to attract top talent away from other opportunities. Score this element a 0 if the Startup claims, "key management will join after funding." Score this element -10 if the founders have failed to attract any talent to commit full time to the project. After all, if key people (those more knowledgeable about the industry) won't commit to the opportunity, would an investor?

Element 5: Business Acumen

What is it?

A survey I conducted years ago[15] showed that it takes a well-balanced management team to run a successful Startup. This team is made up of three elements: Business Acumen, Domain Knowledge and Operational Experience, collectively and colloquially referred to as the Talent Triangle.

The first corner of the Talent Triangle is Business Acumen. Business Acumen, which is typically found in the CEO, COO, and CFO of a company, refers to the team's experience and skills executing business operations (for example, payroll, hiring, tax credits, office rental, etc.). Business Acumen refers to the ability to run the business. Do they know how to budget, to forecast, to lead, to plan? In larger companies Business Acumen will be represented by the CEO or COO of a business.

A founder with Business Acumen will have spent several years doing business at a Startup level (as a lawyer, as a CFO, or as a founder). Business Acumen is leveraged by a Startup to determine: how much money to raise? Where to file **intellectual property**. How and when to hire staff. How and when to **scale**.

Let's take an easy example, Grocery Gateway[16]. Grocery Gateway is an online delivery service for groceries. The Business Domain member of the team at Grocery Gateway would be in charge of trademarking the name, hiring the warehouse staff and raising venture capital. Why does it matter?

Without Business Acumen an opportunity will founder. Companies that run out of capital before realization may be weak in Business Acumen. Business acumen is the result of years of business

---

[15]Sean Wise. "The Talent Triangle." The Globe and Mail, Wednesday, 17 May 2006.
[16]www.grocerygateway.com

experience. It is typically stage-, not domain, centric (i.e., meaning it is less important for Business Acumen to have working in the industry than it is to have worked at a Startup).

Wise entrepreneurs recognize their weaknesses and realize that they are not just asking for money, but also asking for business expertise. A perfect example is David Koetsch, inventor of Grow Zorb[17].

Koetsch is a design engineer and came seeking funding fully understanding his product, his customers and his competition. It was clear to investors that David has Domain Knowledge and operational experience, but lacks Business Acumen. David even mentions in his pitch that part of the reason he is there is to seek out a partner with business knowledge. When funders finally agreed to invest, one of their conditions of the deal was, "We need a person who can run the business in hand, so we've got to develop that person as quickly as possible." Every business needs the three key elements in the Talent Triangle to be successful. As an entrepreneur you need to be fully aware of any weakness in the Talent Triangle, and fix any weakness as soon as possible.

Examples in action

Startup Founder Mr. A has spent ten years as CFO of various Startups. Mr. A is able to answer the business questions raised in the pitch (for example, what is your **Break Even point**?).

At Amazon.com, the founder with Business Acumen would have been responsible for naming the company, filing the trademarks, acquiring the office space, raising seed capital, etc.

---

[17]www.growzorb.com

Questions to ask

Who on the team has worked in a Startup before? Doing what? What resources are leveraged for corporate decisions?

How to score this element:

Score this opportunity a:

- -10 if ...founders have no prior business experience.
- -5 if ...one founder has some minor business experience.
- 0 if ...one founder has lots of business experience.
- 5 if ...all founders have business experience.
- 10 if ...all founders are serial entrepreneurs with successful exits.

How to score this element:

If your team is lean on Business Acumen, recruit lawyers, accountants and financers to raise this element's score.

Element 6: Domain Knowledge

What is it?

The second corner of the Talent Triangle is Domain Knowledge. Domain Knowledge is obtained by working in an industry. **Domain Knowledge** is about knowing your customer and your industry. Does management understand what their customer wants? Do they know how their customer buys? Do they understand what features and benefits are most important to their end user? Domain Knowledge also deals with understanding one's industry. If your Startup was a grocery store, Domain Knowledge would not only help you to sell the food on your shelves, but also how to get that food onto the shelves in the first place.

If you want to run a Startup that revolutionizes banking, Domain Knowledge would come in the form of years of experience working in the financial sector, preferably in banking. The belief behind this element is that in order to implement change, one must have inside knowledge.

A person who is the former COO of Bank of America would be seen to have strong Domain Knowledge at a software firm trying to revolutionize the back end processing of electronic banking transfers.

Domain Knowledge is necessary to understand client needs. Domain Knowledge is needed to fully grasp the sub optimal solution which is generating the opportunity. Domain Knowledge can also help identify and attract key resources and talent as well as help ensure the Startup's go-to-market plan is reasonable and realistic.
At Grocery Gateway, the person who understands not only where to get the food from, but also explicitly understands the end user's needs will cover the Domain Knowledge corner of the Talent Triangle.

Why it matters?

Without Domain Knowledge, Startups are likely to build a solution that no one wants. Worse yet, without Domain Knowledge many Startups oversimplify their problem analysis and may attempt to solve problems that not a concern to industry end users. Without Domain Knowledge, customer needs and industry hurdles may be under-addressed.

TIP: To increase Domain Knowledge, consider forming a BLUE RIBBON PANEL of your future clients. Work with them to test your assumption.

Examples in action

Mr. B spent two decades in the wireless payment industry, most recently as VP of a National Bank. He knows what clients want. He knows the industry's fatal flaws and he sees an opportunity. Mr. B brings Domain Knowledge to Startups in the wireless payment industry.

At Amazon.com a founder with Domain Knowledge would understand the book industry and understand how customers acquire books.

Questions to ask

Who on the team has worked in this industry before? What connections does the management have to the industry? On what did you base your assessment of the client's Pain Point? Which future clients have you run this idea by?

© Sean Evan Wise

How to score this element:

Score this opportunity a:

- -10 if ...no founders have industry experience and no future customers were consulted.
- -5 if ...the only Domain Knowledge has come from future clients.
- 0 if ...one founder has worked in the industry for less than five years.
- 5 if ...at least one or more founders have more than five years in the industry.
- 10 if ...all founders have ten or more years in the industry.

Raising the Score

If your team is lean on Domain Knowledge consider putting together a monthly panel made up of half a dozen industry experts and potential future clients to raise this element's score. Show this user centric panel your product assumptions and development thoughts. Follow the Lean Startup methodology of Build – Measure – Learn.[18]

---

[18]Eris Reis. (2011). The Lean Startup: How Today's Entrepreneurs Use Continuous Innovation to Create Radically Successful Businesses. New York: Crown Business.

Element 7: Operational Experience

What is it?

The third corner of the Talent Triangle is Operational Experience. Entrepreneurs in this corner know how to make and deliver the solution to the customer. In an online grocery store, this corner would supervise not only the creation of the e-commerce front end website, but also the delivery of the food on the back end. This role is usually filled by the CTO or COO.

Operational Experience is all about getting the product from design to delivery. The Domain Knowledge informs you of what features are most important, but the operational experience people know how to not only build it, but they know how to get it into the market. Operational experience is needed to deliver the solution. This corner of the Talent Triangle actually builds and ships things. Operational Experience can only come from doing. At online bookstore Amazon. com, operational experience not only helps them build the web store that sells the books, but also understands how to get those books into the purchaser's hands. If that sounds like a lot, that is because it most certainly is.

Entrepreneurs who have delivered similar solutions to different industries would score high on this element. A founder with Operational Experience will have knowledge on how to not only build the product, but also will understand what it will take to get the product, service or solution into the hands of end users. At Grocery Gateway the Operations Expert will know not only how to accept food orders online, but also how to take electronic payments securely and will also be responsible for determining how many trucks are needed each day.

Why it matters?

Without Operational Experience, founders may never launch. Or worse yet, they may launch but may fail to deliver on their promises. A great product is only great if it reaches the end users.

TIP: To increase Operational Experience, founders should join a trade association or industry group. In many cities, Startup CFOs participate in a quarterly roundtables hosted by one of the "Big 4" accounting firms. Similar associations exist for many Startup roles and even more exist for industry (for example, IT, healthcare). By participating in knowledge transfer with peers, a founder can often get context on their present situation and they can even discover solutions.

Examples in action

Mrs. C has worked in software for many years. She can write relevant code with her eyes closed. Having Mrs. C involved in a software Startup would add operational experience.

At Amazon.com the operational experience corner of the Talent Triangle would not only be responsible for the website but also for the shipping and distribution.

Questions to ask

Who on the team has created and sold similar solutions before? Do you have all the parts you need (resources, people, etc.) to bring your product to market? If not, what remains outstanding?

How to score this element:

Score this opportunity a:

- -10 if ...the team has no operational experience and feels it needs none.
- -5 if ...the team has no operational experience.
- 0 if ...at least one founder has some experience building similar solutions.
- 5 if ...at least one founder has built and delivered similar products.
- 10 if ...the solution has been successfully created sold and delivered to customers.

How to score this element:

If your team lacks Operational Experience and you want to raise the score of this element, you need to bring on staff that has historically built similar products. The ability to build and deliver your product to end users is not something your venture can do without. Operational Experience is not something you can rely on outside advisors for. E.g. if you are building an app for Apple's iPad®, you really do need a founder who knows how to code such

Element 8: Board of Directors/Advisors

What is it?

Often the **Catch 22 of Entrepreneurship** (i.e., To raise money you need a top team but in order to have a top team you need capital) prevents a Startup from attracting top talent full time. This can leave the Startup's Talent Triangle unfulfilled. In order to address weaknesses in management teams, I recommend recruiting a grade A Board.

A good Board serves many purposes. A good Board:

- Provides a sounding board for founders;
- Provides Arms' Length review;
- Expands the network resources available; and
- Expands leadership bandwidth and experience.
- Signals to the world that your venture is worth supporting.

This last point, signalling, is worth exploring further. In economics, **Signalling Theory**[19] is the idea that one party credibly conveys some information about itself to another party. By adding top calibre individuals to your Board, you signal that the venture is worth supporting. When Meg Whitman, the chief executive of Hewlett-Packard and the former chief executive of eBay, joined the Board of Zaarly, a Startup connecting errands with those available to undertake them signalled the market that it was an important venture. After all, most assume Whitman, who led eBay into a worldwide ecommerce success story, knows something about Zaarly's province (i.e., industry) and by joining the ventures she is endorsing such.

---

[19]B.L. Connelly, S.T. Certo, R.D. Ireland, & C. Reutzel. (2011). "Signaling Theory: A Review and Assessment." Journal of Management 37(1):39-65.

Element 9: Social Capital

What is it?

Social networks are made up of the connections in your life (for example, work, personal, school). Social Capital refers to the goodwill trapped inside an entrepreneur's social network. Entrepreneurs with high levels of social capital will be able to "call in favours" to acquire resources and opportunities for the Startup. As discussed, Startups never have enough capital to gather the resources they require. Even if they do have the money, it may not be enough to convince a reporter to cover the story or a customer to allow a pilot or trial run of the solution. Social Capital allows entrepreneurs to leverage their position in the industry/community to the benefit of the Startup.

Why it matters?

In the 21st Century, there is growing literature around the concept of social networks. In the last few decades this literature has explored the benefits and uses of social networks. Most famous of all is the work of Granovetter[20]. Mark Granovetter was interested in how social networks impact job hunting.

In exploring job opportunities and their origins, Granovetter found the majority of job leads came not from your friends and family (e.g., your strong ties) but from friends of your friends (e.g., you weak ties). This became known as the Strength of Weak Ties Theory. This theory argues that you and your friends and family have access to similar information, while weak ties have access to knowledge outside of your social network.

---

[20]Mark S. Granovetter. (1973). "The Strength of Weak Ties." The American Journal of Sociology, 78(6): 1360-1380.

Entrepreneurs who act as social network hubs with lots of weak connections (who bring in new information) and many strong connections (which can help execute on that information and which can help signal success), have a greater ability to obtain key resources (e.g., talent, opportunity, etc.)[21]. Investors tend to back those founders with a proven track record of being able to leverage social capital through social networks.

Investors like to back founders who are Known and In the Know. By Known, I mean recognized in the industry. Entrepreneurs whose reputation for success precedes them are seen by investors as having large reserves of Social Capital that you can leverage. Think:

- Donald Trump for Real Estate;
- Elon Musk for Transportation; or
- Jim Treliving for Food Franchise.

Having a member of your Startup who is Known will not only lead to better media attention (which is cheaper than advertising) but will also increase how others (clients, investors, future employees) view the Startup. If your real estate software Startup attracts Donald Trump to its Board of Directors, others may look at your venture positively based on this point alone. The logic behind this benefit goes like this:

1. Trump Knows how to make money in Real Estate;
2. This Startup has no proof of concept, but
3. If Trump thinks it is worth his time, perhaps it is worth mine?

Being **In the Know** is slightly different. Being in the Know is a form of Domain Knowledge. Knowing the inside track of who does what can help a Startup succeed by leveraging social capital through **back channels**.

---

[21]Michel Ferrary & Mark Granovetter. (2009). "The Role of Venture Capital Firms in Silicon Valley's Complex Innovation Network." Economy and Society 38(2): 326-359.

Examples in action

Mark Zuckerberg is the founder of Facebook, the world's foremost social network. If a social shopping Startup came to me for funding with Mark on the Board, I would definitely score it high in Known & In the Know. In doing so, the Startup in question would be seen as having a **Halo effect** from Mark (for more see Element 32). The halo effect and social capital in general create a Signalling Effect (see Signalling Theory) impacts the way the venture is perceived by others.

Questions to ask

What connections to industry does your team have? Have members of your team been featured on panels or keynotes at industry conferences or media stories? What advantage do you think your prior activities and relationships give the venture?

How to score this element:

Score this opportunity a:

- -10 if ...the team has no prior activity or relationships in the field.
- -5 if ...the team is loosely connected.
- 0 if ...the team has external relationships that might enhance the Startup.
- 5 if ...the founders are well connected in their industry.
- 10 if ...many positive stories appear about the founders in media (use Google to research them).

How to score this element:

To increase this score, increase your social capital. You do that in any number of ways, including by not limited to: joining an industry association, publishing a blog, or attending and actively participating in trade conferences.

Element 10: Team History/Dynamics

What is it?

The only thing investors value more than serial entrepreneurs is serial management teams. A team of founders that has worked together is a treasure. A team of founders who have previously taken a Startup to greatness is the greatest treasure of all.

Even if the new venture is entering a realm previously unknown to the entrepreneurs, investors will value their prior history heavily.
It takes a team to succeed in the world of Startups and a team is more than its constituent parts. Good management teams have a good working dynamic. In fact, testing the level of friction in the management team is a key part of **Due Diligence**.

Opportunity evaluators are key to witness how the founders interact with each other. A team that doesn't have friction may not have it what it takes to make the hard decisions. For maximum success, it is widely believed that a team should have a certain level of internal friction. The friction should be challenging enough to ensure all decisions are thoroughly vetted, but amicable enough to overcome the daily grind of Startup life.

Why it matters?

As with serial entrepreneurs, a team with prior work history generates confidence for investors. Investors believe that team dynamics are crucial for success and having a team with a proven track record helps address the issue of Management Risk (see A few words about Risk in the opening pages of this book).

Examples in Action

YouTube founders Chad Hurley and Steve Chen sold their video Startup to Google for more than US$1.5 billion. So it is no surprise that investors (and media) paid attention on September 12, 2011 when the duo decided to take over flailing social bookmark venture, Delicious. Similarly, when the franchise czars behind Boston Pizza (Jim Treliving and George Melville) took over Mr. Lube, the world noticed.

How to score this element:

Score this opportunity a:

- -10 if ...founders contradict or interrupt each other.
- -5 if ...there is too much friction between the team.
- 0 if ...some founders have a prior history together.
- 5 if ...all founders have worked together.
- 10 if ...all founders have worked together for 5+ years and had a success.

Pain

After people comes pain. Solving a painful problem is the driving force behind most Startups. According to business school Dean, Roger Martin[22], Entrepreneurs seek to drive profits by addressing **sub optimal solutions**. The telephone was better than the telegraph, but was less impactful than the adoption of email. The move to a more optimal level of happiness comes from addressing an unmet need. Yes, telegraphs allowed for remote instant communication, but the telephone allowed for the voice of the sender to be heard and thus provide more context for communication. The innovation cycle continues. Years later, email allowed for remote communications to go from voice to text. The mail system was sub optimal to the email network. Another example, video on demand solved the pain of forgetting to return your movies to the Blockbuster Movie Rental store.

---

[20]Mark S. Granovetter. (1973). "The Strength of Weak Ties." The American Journal of Sociology, 78(6): 1360-1380.

Element 11: Compelling Unmet Need

What is it?

A colleague of mine once noted that all business should focus on addressing an underserved pain. As a result, all Startups should focus on providing a valuable solution to a **unmet pain point**. For Startups in the B2B space (i.e., Startups selling solutions to businesses), most pain points either attempt to increase revenues or mitigate a cost for the customer. For Startups in the B2C space (Startups selling directly to individual end users), the goal is often either to alleviate a pain or increase some pleasure.

From a B2C perspective, Google helps address the pain of too much clutter on the Internet. It does this by helping people search and find what they are looking for. From a B2B perspective, Google (AdWords) helps drive revenue by helping businesses connect with those customers searching for their solution.

Why it matters?

The bigger the pain, the more likely your solution is to resonate with customers. Big pain can mean: (a) a small cost solution with a large market (for example, aspirin for headaches); or (b) a large cost solution with a niche market. In some rare cases, the pain can both be large cost and have a large market. This theory argues that you and your friends and family have access to similar information, while weak ties have access to knowledge outside of your social network.

Questions to Ask

What is the goal of the venture? What problem is your team trying to solve? Who experiences such pain? Before your solution is available what are your future customers using to solve this problem? What is the cost of the next best solution? How does such cost compare to the cost of your solution?

How to score this element:

Score this opportunity a:

- -10 if ...no unmet pain exists.
- -5 if ...there is a pain but solutions already exist
- 0 if ...there may be a pain point, but the market has not confirmed.
- 5 if ...the pain point is clear, prevalent and large but unproven.
- 10 if ...early sales confirm that the pain point is clear, prevalent and large.

Element 12: Size of the Pain

What is it?

Pain is the starting point. Without a large unmet problem, it will be difficult for innovative Startups to garner market **traction**. In fact, the larger the pain, the more quickly people will adopt the solution. Look at the extreme rates of adoption behind recent solutions: Facebook (solving the pain of staying in touch with an ever increasing circle of friends); Kindle (solving the pain of having to carry heavy books with you); or even email (solving the pain of having to send written communication by post). This is the one time where large pain is good.

Why it matters?

If the pain doesn't impact enough people, or doesn't impact such people deeply, it will be difficult to gain market traction. If current solutions are seen as good enough, then the pain may not be enough to justify the need for the Startup's solution.

Generally, the larger the pain, the more revenue can be charged for it. Generally, the larger the number of people suffering from such pain, the larger the **total addressable market** (TAM) becomes.

Examples in Action

Compare: Headaches vs. HIV. The market for headache relief is large. That's because the whole world population is susceptible to this inconvenient ailment. HIV, while 100x more impactful, has a smaller total addressable market as less people are struck (as compared to headaches) but the effect is much more grave.

Both headaches and HIV would be said to have large addressable markets, but HIV should generate a score on this element a +10, while aspirin (headache solution) would only receive a +5. The reason? The demand to fight HIV is inelastic (users would pay almost anything to access a solution) while the demand for aspirin is more elastic (would you pay $25 for an aspirin?).

As a rule of thumb, to scope the aggregate Size of the Pain, ask yourself first: How many people suffer from this Pain? Then multiply this number (the TAM) by the intensity of the problem (the size of the pain felt by each user).

Questions to Ask

What is the goal of the venture? What problem is your team trying to solve? Who experiences such pain? Before your solution is available what are your future customers using to solve this problem? What is the cost of the next best solution? How does such cost compare to the cost of your solution?

How to score this element:

This is more than a simple quantitative calculation. As a starting point, mentally scope the size of the market (for example, millions of people exercise) and multiply that number by the cost of the solution (for example, running shoes cost $200 on average). This will give you a thumbnail sketch of the size of the pain.

Score this opportunity a:

- -10 if …there is no unmet need.
- -5 if …the need is small and the market is niche.
- 0 if …the market is global but the unmet need is small.
- 5 if …the market is niche but the pain is large.
- 10 if …the unmet need is huge and the total addressable market is global.

Raising the Score

To increase this element's score, ask yourself if any other end users are possible to focus on. Ask yourself if there are other possible uses for your solution, service or product. See if any of these other options (users or uses) lead to a higher pain point. For example, Viagra® as a heart medication addressed a smaller pain point than Viagra® as a solution for erectile dysfunction.

Element 13: Intensity of Pain

What is it?

HIV is more damaging than a headache. So the solution for HIV addresses a larger pain point than aspirin. Generally, the bigger the issue, the more people will pay for the solution and the quicker that solution will be adopted in the market. This is the basis around the concept of: **Elasticity of Demand**.

Elasticity relates to both price and demand. The more inelastic the demand, the more a buyer will be willing to pay to acquire it. If a product's demand is inelastic, then customers simply must have it. For example, your need to breathe makes the demand for oxygen incredibility inelastic; therefore, you would pay any price to breathe. If the demand for a product is elastic, then it is very price sensitive (for example, you might be willing to pay $1.00 for a fresh apple; but it is unlikely you would be willing to pay $50.00 for that same apple). The more elastic the demand, the more impact price changes will have on demand.

Why it matters?

Consumers have limited income. As a result, most prioritize their needs based on inelasticity (for example, most students would buy groceries to eat before they bought tickets to a concert, since the need to eat is more inelastic than the need to see live music). The inelastic the demand for a Startup's solution, the more that Startup can charge for the solution and the more that solution will be seen as a "must have" item. Not just a "nice to have item".

Questions to Ask

Why do people buy what you are selling? What drives their desire? How would classify that desire: is it a need or a want?

How to score this element:

Startups whose products are inelastic score high on this element. The more critical a Startup's solution, the higher it scores on this element. Based on this, score this opportunity a:

- -10 if ...the demand is completely elastic.
- -5 if ...the problem has high elasticity of demand and is thus very price sensitive (e.g., customers would buy it for $1.00 but not for $1.10).
- 0 if ...the market is global but the demand elasticity is high.
- 5 if ...many third parties have identified this market has having an intense, unmet pain. The demand for a solution is strong.
- 10 if ...the demand for the Startup's solution is 100% inelastic (i.e., customers will pay any price for it).

---

[23]J.A Timmons. (1994). "Opportunity Recognition: The Search for Higher Potential Ventures," in Bygrave, W.D (ed), The Portable MBA in Entrepreneurship, 26-54, Toronto: John Wiley & Sons.

Element 14: Durability of the Opportunity

What is it?

According to modern scholars[23], an opportunity has four key elements. It must be:

1) Attractive: it has to offer a 10x better solution.
2) Timely: the market is ready to buy what you are selling.
3) Durable: the opportunity must last long enough to crystalize the potential (i.e., it has to last long enough for you to sell your solution).
4) Value adding: it offers a solution seen as valuable to potential customers.

In 2008, after Barack Obama was elected president and "Yes We Can!" T-shirts were in demand as Americans wanted to wear them to show their support. Two years later, with the President's approval rating at an all-time low, these shirts couldn't be given away at any price. Thus the opportunity for "Yes We Can!" T-shirts might have been seen as timely, but not as durable.

One of the scenes in the movie Back to the Future has time traveling protagonist Marty McFly playing Johnny B. Goode at a 1955 high school prom. His audience is dancing away to every beat of his song, the band members have big smiles on their faces and he's captivated his audience. Then Marty starts shredding his guitar, sliding across the stage, jumping from the speakers and crawling along the floor— and as soon as he hits the high note, he realizes his audience is staring at him with a look of horror and shock. And then he says, "I guess you guys aren't ready for that, but your kids are gonna love it."

At the start of the 21st Century, Facebook timed their product launches perfectly to coincide with the general population's readiness for social networking, and they turned the industry into a hot market. Hot markets are always a great thing to be a part of because they can lead to such intense demand that frantic buyers are fighting over products. Even if you're not the top business in a hot market, you're still going to do well. This is a dream come true for any business owner.

In other words: **Timing is Everything**. Rock and Roll was a hot new trend in 1955, however shredding the guitar and jumping off speakers wasn't widely adopted and accepted until the mid-1980s after Punk and Heavy Metal made those practices part of the rock experience. When launching a new business, the best scenario is one in which you can be a part of a market that is on the verge of turning hot. The timing has to be perfect—not too early and not too late. Returning to our example of social networking sites, remember that before Facebook and Myspace, there was Friendster. This site launched in 2003 and quickly adopted 3 million users, but they were still too new for the general population and thus fell behind Facebook when it overtook its competitors.

How do you spot hot markets?

Through the news, water-cooler chat and walking down the street and paying attention to people's behaviours. The signs of changing trends are everywhere. A useful online tool is Google Trends which lists the top 100 most searched terms in the past day. It's a great way to see what people are interested in. Almost every night on the news I hear about the spread of swine flu across the world. I'm sure any business selling products that help fight swine flu is doing really well right now. Some other big trends occurring today are:

- Anything to do with seniors, as the baby boom generation is

---

[24]www.tidytrailers.com

retiring
- Anything in mobile and iPhone applications
- Hygiene products
- Fuel-efficient cars
- Junk removal

The two entrepreneurs from *Tidy Trailers*[24] are certainly part of a bigger trend: junk removal. Even as a small business with low brand recognition, the hot market is probably one of the reasons why the company was able to bring in good revenue. People simply have too much stuff and this provides a hot business opportunity.

Why it matters?

In today's global, competitive, and rapidly innovating environment one must not only be quick to market to capture demand, but founders must ensure that demand will be durable enough to allow the Startup to profit from it. After all, solutions to the Y2K problem had very little value in 2001.

Any entrepreneur jumping into a hot market is more likely to succeed because there are already customers waiting to buy. So always be aware of how hot or cold your market is and how its timeliness will affect your business.

Questions to Ask

What evidence do you have that the market will wait for your solution? Who else is working on this problem? How are along are your direct competitors?

How to score this element:

- -10 if ...the solution is a fad.
- -5 if ...the opportunity will last less than two years.

- 0 if ...the durability of the opportunity is unknown.
- 5 if ...the opportunity has been around and unmet for a long time.
- 10 if ...the demand is durable.

How to score this element:

Alternative uses for your product, service or solution may lead to longer durability. So to increase this score, don't be afraid to mention your **Plan B**.

Product/Solution

Why do/will people pay you? Do you offer a product that is ten times better than what is currently available in the market? Does your service mitigate a huge pain point? Does your solution offer value to the end user? To the customer?

Product is as import as Pain, so this group of elements carries the same weight in the WiseGuide™. This section assumes there is a large demand or need for the solution, it also assumes you can deliver on your goals. So it assumes a fully working product exists.

Element 15: The 10x Rule

What is it?

In order to overcome market incumbents, new solutions must be 10x better. This is at the heart of **the 10x Rule**. Being a slightly better, faster, stronger, more cost efficient is not enough. In order to attract customers away from their current means of addressing the pain, your new solution must be 10x better than the current solution.

Once you have an idea that someone will be willing to pay for, how do you improve it so that everyone is willing to pay for it? Begin looking at every possible way to make the idea so much better that it satisfies the 10x Rule. The 10x Rule means that in order to gain market traction a product must be exponentially better than the incumbent solutions in that it is. 10 times faster, 10 times smaller, 10 times cheaper, and 10 times more profitable.

The reason for this rule: Market adoption. Historically, being a little better isn't enough to gain huge market share fast. Now compare that to some other improvements we have seen:

- Email is WAY faster than snail mail. Email is a successful product.
- Air travel is WAY faster than train. Air travel is a successful product.
- Mp3 players can hold WAY more than CD players. Mp3 player is a successful product.

Examples in Action

Email was so widely adopted in such a short timeframe because it was 10x faster than traditional mail, so much so that traditional postal service is colloquially now referred to as snail mail. Wikipedia has 10x the articles as Encyclopaedia Britannica. Amazon has 10x the number of books as the World's Largest Brick & Mortar Bookstore (located in downtown Toronto, my home town). Apple's iPod™ holds more than 10x the songs of any Sony Walkman™. Obviously, this is an oversimplification. In most, if not all these cases, the product diffused because of its quick integration into the demands of an ever evolving productive lifestyle. Email is better than mail because it is instant and because it allows social distance (less intimate and iterative that the phone), Wikipedia is better than the encyclopaedia because it is a shared, free, editable resource, not because it is just 10x bigger, and so on.

Why it matters?

Being incrementally innovative is not sufficient. A little better is not good enough. A little cheaper won't move customers to adopt. In all but a few markets, the pain your solution addresses is being addressed. E.g. Yes, email is faster than snail mail. But the telegraph was already a faster way to communicate.

Most of your potential customers have already some form of solution in place. Next best is often good enough. The rate of adoption of a new product is directly correlated to the quantum of innovation being proposed. The 10x rule implies that **exponentially better solutions are required to overcome the impact of sunk costs.**[25]

If you already bought a non-returnable iPad 1 on sale and then the next month a newer version, say the iPad 2, is released. In most cases, the newer version would have to be at least 10x better to make a customer want to purchase it. This is less an issue of price, and more an issue of cognitive dissonance. The concept of **sub optimal solutions** is also at play here. Killer ideas, those that totally change the status quo are called disruptive.

---

[25]Grant Cardon. (2011). The 10X Rule: The Only Difference Between Success and Failure. Toronto: Wiley.

© Sean Evan Wise

Amazon.com was a disruptive Startup in that it offered book lovers more than 100x the number of titles. Amazon literally changed the book selling landscape further when it launched the Kindle™. Prior to Amazon.com's arrival, book lovers options were sub optimal. Amazon.com disrupted the landscape by addressing a sub optimal solution. In doing so, the founders were able to trigger not only rapid and mass adoption, they were also able to extract large economic rents by capturing the unmet needs of the book lover.

In fact, this exponential level of disruption is referred to by entrepreneurial scholars as **Creative Destruction**, and according to Schumpeter, this lies at the heart of true entrepreneurial innovation[26].

How to score this element:

- -10 if …the solution is indistinguishable from its next market competitor or the status quo.
- -5 if …it is a only slightly better, faster, etc.
- 0 if …the quantum of innovation is unknown.
- 5 if …it is significantly better, but there is no evidence of true market demand.
- 10 if …according to customers Is it 10x better, stronger, aster, more valuable?

---

[26]Joseph Schumpeter and Ursula Back. (2003). "The Theory of Economic Development." The European Heritage in Economics and the Social Sciences, 1, 61-116.

Element 16: Innovation Origin

What is it?

If a product wasn't created by the Startup, most investors will not invest. Regardless that an entrepreneur might have exclusive license to sell such an object in that country, if your main solution, product or service is not created by the founders, most investors will call a **hard stop**.

Why it matters?

The reason should be obvious: future research and development, or R&D. If the Startup is able to attract a customer base, what will the Startup sell next? From where will new ideas come?

Examples in Action

Microsoft® in the late 1990s was famous for having an internal attitude against products not developed in house by Microsoft®. This bias is commonly referred to as "Not Invented Here[27]" syndrome or simply "NIH". For many years it was believed that Microsoft's expansion would be the result of internal R&D.

Compare this to Google who not only grew revenue through internal R&D development (e.g., Gmail) but also through Startup acquisition (e.g., YouTube). As discussed later (Element 30) acquisitions are one way large companies expand their product and services.

---

[27]http://en.wikipedia.org/wiki/Not_Invented_Here

Questions to Ask

How did you come up with this? Who invented it? What are they working on next?

How to score this element:

- -10 if ...the solution was licensed.
- -5 if ...the solution is a global exclusive license.
- 0 if ...the solution is not propriety
- 5 if ...the inventor works at the Startup but is not fully vested (e.g., he isn't a shareholder of the Startup) in the venture.
- 10 if ...the inventor is an active, full time founder in the business.

© Sean Evan Wise

Element 17: IP status

What is it?

Intellectual property (IP) is a subset of commercial law. IP grants the holder (usually the inventor) the exclusive right to produce and reap the benefits from such for limited period of time (in some cases more than 25 years). There are many types of IP (for example, trademarks, copyrights), but for most entrepreneurs the patent is the key to protecting their IP.

A patent is granted by a country's patent office. Every country's IP laws are different, but generally: A patent is granted if an innovation is seen (by a government inspector) to have novelty, utility and non-obviousness. A patent allows the owner exclusive rights to do a particular thing in a particular way for a limited time. A patent gives the holder the exclusive right to monetize their innovation. After a set number of years (which may differ by country), the patent will expire and the solution becomes public domain meaning that anyone can reproduce it without permission. Solutions in the public domain allow anyone to utilize the innovation for commercial gain.

Similarly a trademark (for example, Nike's Just Do It!) gives the owner the exclusive right to use that phrase. Both may require filing with the federal government to ensure your rights are declared, approved and protected. Typically it is best to register your IP before showing it the general public (or going on national television). In the case of patents, going on television and disclosing your technology to the world before filing would not be wise, in fact doing so may invalidate your ability to get a patent at all.

To that end, most investors prefer entrepreneurs first talk to their lawyers and file all the paperwork to protect their intellectual property before seeking capital.

Why it matters?

IP is meant to reward the holders with the sole right to monetize the innovation and recoup monies invested. Some argue that IP is necessary to facilitate commercial investment. Others feel that IP laws are out-dated and actually hinder innovation.

But what if all you have is a good idea but it is not a proprietary patentable technology? Well let's be clear, ideas aren't protectable. Having a good idea is not enough. Would we pay James Cameron for his ideas of Titanic and Avatar? Or would we pay for a ticket to see the movie? It was Cameron's execution, not his ideas that won him Oscars. The same is true for investments. It is the execution of the idea that has value, not the idea itself.

Examples in Action

If Inventor Ms. D. invents a new way of curing student lateness, she may file for a patent. It would give her, and only her, the right to sell solutions based on her invention. It would also publish her solution and provide to the public information about how her innovation works.

Questions to Ask

What is proprietary about your solution? Who invented it? When was the patent filed? Registered? Granted? What exactly is yours and yours alone to do?

How to score this element:

- -10 if ...the solution is not proprietary.
- -5 if ...the solution is proprietary but the IP has not yet been filed.

- 5 if …there multiple patents filed globally.
- 10 if …there are multiple patents GRANTED globally.

Raising the Score

Finally a patent is often cost prohibitive (could cost upwards of $25,000 per patent) and often unenforceable (due to the Startup's lack of resources). Notwithstanding, filing for a patent or other forms of IP, can add more value to the venture than they cost. Furthermore, it can take many years to have a patent processed (and rejected) during such time, a venture with many "patents pending" is seem more valuable than a venture without IP. So file what you can to raise this element's score.

Element 18: Key Asset Access

What is it?

Some solutions require access to specific and explicit scarce commodities. For example, high school gymnasiums can only be rented out to one group at a time. If a group had monopolistic control over the rent charged, they would score high on this element. Likewise, if a necessary asset is scarce or, worse yet, dependent on access provided by a monopolizing group (for example, oil because it requires skilled people with special equipment to extract and refine), the score would fall.

Why it matters?

Scarcity drives most pricing. If your solution depends on the product of another, then your venture is exposed to risk. Risk that could result in downward margin pressure.

Examples in Action

GUATS[28] makes the world's softest pyjamas. Their BamJamz™ are made from bamboo. If there should be a shortage of bamboo, their business would be greatly affected.

A call centre typically requires access to minimum wage employees. A mobile software app developer requires programmers with knowledge and experience with mobile software. A shortage of either of these human resources would exert downward pressure on profit margins.

---

[28]www.guats.com

Questions to Ask

What factors in your solution are crucial? What could get in the way of your product's success?

How to score this element:

- -10 if ...the solution is completely dependent on a scarce resource.
- -5 if ...the solution is dependent on a semi scarce resource.
- 0 if ...key assets are not involved in this opportunity.
- 5 if ...the solution requires a very commonly available substance or resource.
- 10 if ...the company has everything it needs and the solution requires nothing vital externally.

Raising the Score

Any exclusive claim on key assets will raise this elements score. Similarly, if you are able to lock up the pricing for key resources before large demand sets in, you may be able to garner a competitive advantage through this element.

Element 19: Proof of Concept

What is it?

All entrepreneurs believe in the possibility of their success. To gain objective perspective, investors often seek a third party's arm's length evidence that your product is valuable. Every entrepreneur that has stood before investors thinks that they have a great business idea and it will make millions of dollars. When you have invested a lot of time and money into a business idea you're likely going to think it's worth the investment. The result is the entrepreneur has a biased perception of the business idea, which is why every entrepreneur must find a way to prove that their business idea will turn a profit.

The best way to convince an investor that people will be willing to buy your product is by waving a big sales order in front of them. In other words, get customers now, even before you have built your product. How can you possibly get a sales order without having built anything? It can be done, and some of the most successful entrepreneurs are the ones who can make a sale on just an idea. One way to do so is by providing the customer an incentive for taking the risk of purchasing your product so early. A common example is condominium builders who sell units even before a shovel has broken the ground. All they have to show the customers are concept pictures, an empty lot and a very good salesperson. In turn, the customer can purchase the condo at a discounted price for taking the risk that the condo may not be built exactly as promised. Some of the other main advantages to gain customers early in the process are:

- Offsets the cost of building the product. You automatically get cash in hand with interest accumulating in the bank.

---

[29]www.pointerware.com

- Reduces the need to seek out financing from investors.
- Provides a growing number of users who can provide feedback.
- Confirms there is a need for this product.

When two engineers pitched Softshell Computers[29], investors were quick to tell them how ridiculous the idea seemed. As soon as one of their customers provided investors with her testimony of how their product has cut down on her house cleaning because she spends all her time using their product, the Dragons were sold too. You can be assured you're onto something big if you're able to make this early sale at pretty much any price. If a customer is willing to pay for your product at any price, than that's excellent evidence that the demand for this product is extremely high. It is also excellent motivation for you and others to build the product as quickly as possible. In economic terms this means that the price is inelastic and this term brings smiles to investor faces.

Even if you're unable to make any sales this early, letters of intent are better than nothing. An entrepreneur is always selling their business idea—to customers, investors, employees, partners, and even to their spouses. Your word that your idea is great can only go so far, but showing evidence will prove it.

Why it matters?

The best proof of concept is sales. Sales show that demand for the product exists but early sales do much more. With early sales, entrepreneurs:

1) Can directly engage with future user to evolve solutions.
2) Can lower their dependence on external capital.
3) Can validate assumptions in the revenue model.

Sales are not the only form of proof of concept. Other third party endorsements can be garnered from a venture's corporate partnerships, investor list and early adopters. Often there is so much uncertainty at play in innovation, reviewers are wise to look everywhere and anywhere for additional validation.

Examples in Action

During an annual venture fair (for example, where companies come to pitch a panel of investors) I once watched a bombastic venture capitalist loudly, and in a very public manner, inform a presenter the fallibility of their venture. He stood up and yelled from the judge's table: "This is a stupid idea. No one will buy it. How do you even know anyone cares enough to buy it?" The entrepreneurs' answer was calm, confident and much less loud. The berated founder simply replied: "Because we sold 10,000 units in the first 90 days". Nothing says proof of concept like actual sales.

Questions to Ask?

Other than the founders and family, who else believes in this venture? What proof do you have that anybody cares about your solution?

How to Score this Element

This element is fairly easy to score. The more reliable, external, reputable the source of the evidence presented is, the higher the score.

- -10 if …only the founders and family have seen the solution in action.
- -5 if …partners, investors, etc. have shown confidence in the opportunity.
- 0 if …the solution has been deployed but is in the pilot stage.

- 5 if ...the solution has been sold to early adopters the founders are still working on improvements and expansion.
- 10 if ...founders have a long history of sales, and sales continue to grow.

Raising the Score

The best proof of concept, the most compelling evidence that your product, service or solution is needed, is sales revenue. Nothing is more compelling proof than actual customers buying actual solutions.

But what if it is too early to generate sales from this opportunity? Well in that case, you can raise this element's score by generating third party evidence through alternate means. These means might include: endorsements, focus groups, corporate partnerships, strategic investments, shared go to market plans, etc. Anything that shows reviewers you are not alone in believing this opportunity is great, will go far to increase this element's score.

Element 20: Revenue

What is it?

In real estate the mantra is location, location, location. In entrepreneurship the mantra is sell, sell, sell. Prior to the dot.com bubble bursting a decade ago, proof of concept was seen to be: turn the light switch on ⇨ light goes on.

Today, more and more investors have expanded the proof of concept definition to be: turn the light switch on ⇨ light goes on ⇨ customer pays $5/hour to read under it.

In today's world of Agile Development, the mantra is fail fast; fail often. Innovations are tested against the market as soon as possible. If the market doesn't want to pay for what a venture is selling, then is there a need for that innovation.

Why it matters?

Nothing helps an opportunity succeed like success! Revenue means the solution is valued by end users. Revenue can also generate secondary benefits, including:

- Early and direct access to customer feedback;
- Validation of assumptions in the revenue model;
- A deeper understanding what it will take to sell and scale the solution.

Questions to Ask?

Have you sold your product/solution/service? What was the total revenue over the last 18 months? Were they early sales or more standardized replicable sales? What is needed to really scale up scales? What would it take to double sales to date in 90 days?

How to Score this Element

- -10 if ...the Startup is 18 months or more from being able to scale revenue.
- -5 if ...the Startup is less than 18 months away from first revenue.
- 0 if ...the solution has been sold, but not enough to be standardized.
- 5 if ...they have enough monthly revenue to break-even.
- 10 if ...they have their costs covered and are making a small profit.
- 25 if ...they have not only positive cash flow but they have been quantifiably profitable for more than six months.

Element 21: Strong Margins

What is it?

Margin is an accounting concept representing a percentage of the difference between the cost of making a product and its price. Margin represents how much profit you make from the sale of each unit. Strong margins refer to both margins that are large and margins that are sustainable.

Accounting terms, including: **EBITA, breakeven point and COGS** should be familiar to all opportunity evaluators. If they are not, flip to the Glossary section and familiarize yourself with them.

The core value of margins lies in to additional accounting concepts: **ARPU and CoCA**. ARPU (**average revenue per user**) helps to determine how much revenue each new customer brings in. If you are selling an app on iTunes™ the ARPU would be gross sales divided by the number of users. If you are selling business legal services, the ARPU would be calculated using this equation: total hours billed in revenue divided by number of corporate clients served. In a nutshell, ARPU represents how much extra you make each time you add a new client.

CoCA (**cost of client acquisition**) is a similarly calculated figure, this time based on Total Sales & Marketing costs for the year divided by the number of new clients acquired.

Notwithstanding these formulas, this element does not require you to quantitatively calculate the net profits. You need not have all the information either. Instead, simply look to the top level margins to ensure that ARPU always swamps CoCA (for example, the amount to acquire a new user is significantly less than the money that client brings to the venture).

Why it matters?

Large margins are good. They afford the entrepreneur flexibility. They allow for greater price flexibility which in turn protects against opportunities that have demand elasticity (i.e., if you have small margins, you need ample demand). But extremely large margins are attractive. And large margins can attract competition as others try to can mine the opportunity.

Innovators often look to elements like: huge market potential, first mover advantage, network effects, etc. But good innovators also recognize the role margins play.

Examples in Action

If grocery store buys apples at $1 a bag and sells those same apples an hour later for $2, the margin on apples is 50%. If that same store buys apples the next day for $2 a bag and sells those same apples an hour later for $3 the margin that day is 33%. The drop in margin not only raised the risk (in the first case if you couldn't resell the apples you would be out only $1, but in the second case, your loss would double). In the world of opportunity evaluation, you always seek higher margins. Higher margins allow for more stability in uncertain economies by providing wiggle room on the price.

An entrepreneur pitched investors: *Tan on the Run*[30], a mobile tanning business. She has been making good profits so far and was hoping to franchise her business. Investors were concerned that it would be difficult to scale her business because the cost to service each customer was fairly high.

As Shark Tank investor Kevin O'Leary told her: "All the cost of going there, setting up time, then going back, is built into your price.

---

[30]www.tanontherun.com

That means you're making 30% less than if I set this up on a corner somewhere. You're charging the same and you're doing all this extra work. If you had a fixed location you could line them up like cattle and spray them down."

Investors are seeking investments that can scale because they want 5 to 10 times the return on the amount of money they've invested. Tan on the Run is a great business for one entrepreneur but with the low profit margin, it will face challenges when it tries to scale towards franchises. When you hear investors mention scalability, they're really talking about how much potential a business has to make a lot of money.

Questions to Ask?

What are your gross margins? Your EBITA? How do you mark up (i.e., place a margin on) your product? What are the cost of the goods being sold? What do you buy your resources (for example, talent, food, lumber) at? At what price are you selling your solution? Do others (e.g., retailers) mark up your solution?

How to Score this Element

Give this element a:

- -10 if ...margins are less than 20% or if CoCA < ARPU
- -5 if ...margins are less than 50%.
- 0 if ...margins are fluctuating and not yet stable enough to evaluate.
- 5 if ...margins are less than 100%. ARPU is much larger than CoCA.
- 10 if ...the solution has huge margins, greater than 100%. ARPU is 10x CoCA.

Raising the Score

To increase this element's score, really focus on the following formula:

> # CoCA < ARPU
>
> Cost to find clients must be less than the revenue from clients

Consider business models that will lower CoCA or boost ARPU. To lower CoCA one might deploy **Gorilla Marketing** techniques or engage in **viral marketing**. Anything that gets potential customers to try before they buy will potentially drive CoCA down in the long run (although in the short run it may have the opposite effect). To increase the ARPU consider the theory of **Double Dipping**. Double Dipping refers to the ability to:

- Build the product, service, solution once;
- Bill for it twice; and
- Generate revenue three times.

The author of this book was able to Double Dip when he worked on Dragons' Den for five seasons. He was paid to support the show; then paid again to give keynote speeches about the show; then paid again to transform his experience into content for this book, effectively double dipping (actually, triple dipping might be more accurate).

To raise the score on this element brainstorm ways to double dip. Can you sell upgrades? Can you switch to a recurring revenue model ($9.99/month instead of $99.99 onetime)? Will users want refills or extras? Could you sell the same product to another market? All of these efforts, done well, would raise this element's score.

Element 22: Scalability

What is it?

Scalability refers to an opportunity's potential to bring in top line revenue faster than the growth of related costs. Put another way, the margins (see Element 23: Margins) grow as volumes grow . Online software as a service is extremely scalable. Facebook™ adds thousands of new members each day, but each new member does not cost very much because of the sheer number of members over which that cost is amortized). Professional services (e.g., lawyer) are not very scalable. For a lawyer to make more money from his revenue model, he must either: (a) work more hours or (b) charge more per hour. Legal services do not scale, since increases in volume do not necessarily lead to large product savings.

Scalability has a lot to do variable costs. Fixed Costs refer to expenses that are incurred no matter how many units are produced/sold. Filing a patent (see Element 18: IP) is a fixed cost. The legal fees on the patent filing are the same if the company filing sells one, many or none of the patent's subject.

Variable Costs are expenses dependant on the number of units sold. The amount of steel used by Toyota Motors is a variable cost. The more cars they make, the more steel needed, the greater the cost. In theory, to be scalable means to have relatively small variable costs. Downloadable software is extremely scalable, since once the application is developed, a fixed cost, the cost to sell, to distribute and to reproduce (the variable costs) fall almost to zero. Contrast the scalable software domain with the virtually non-scalable professional services domain.

Law services are not scalable, since the revenue model for law is: number of hours billable X average hourly billable rate X number of lawyers working.

In order for a lawyer to drive greater revenue, she must do one of three things:

- work more billable hours; or
- raise her hourly rate; or
- hire more associates.

This means that revenue and costs will grow in sync. This in turn undermines a lawyer's ability to scale.

Why it matters?

Scalability is the key to innovation. For a product to be rapidly and widely adopted the variable costs should be relatively low. An **Economy of Scale** is a macroeconomic concept that refers to the cost advantages garnered by expansion. Some factors of production can lead to a decrease in the average per unit cost of production. Literally, by making more of the solution the company makes better margins.

How to Score this Element

Give this element a:

- -10 if ...there are no economies of scale to be had.
- -5 if ...there are few economies of scale to leverage.
- 0 if ...scalability is unproven due to few sales.
- 5 if ...the solution is moderately scalable.
- 10 if ...the solution is very scalable.

© Sean Evan Wise

Province

Province refers to what industry the Startup works in. Province refers to the portfolio of elements that reflect the domain or market the Startup competes in. Industries can be general (footwear) or specific (athletic footwear) or even niche (skateboard street sneakers). Most companies intrinsically know what industry they are in, but they aren't always correct.

In the WiseGuide™, Province elements comprise, in aggregate, 20% of the overall opportunity score.

What industry do you think Google is in? Most say they are in the Search Engine industry. But are they really? I would argue that Google is in the advertising industry. A majority of Google revenue comes from Adwords and "eyeballs" because they provide space for advertising on their web pages.

If you aren't sure about the industry, I recommend looking on federal level websites or simply Google: "Industry" & "Classifications" and look through the relevant list.

Element 23: Market Stage

What is it?

You've just created the best product in the world. Perhaps millions of people could benefit from using your product. It's easy for your friends and family to learn about your concept, but how does the rest of the world find out? Unless you're in the movie Field of Dreams, if you build it doesn't mean that people will start lining up outside your house to buy it. You will need a marketing plan and a strategy to convince the masses to purchase your product.

Rogers' **Diffusion of Innovations theory** outlines that there are five different groups of people who adopt new products at different points in time. Rogers' Theory of Innovation Diffusion[32] attempts to classify product adoption along a curve representing several distinct stages (Innovators, Early Adopters, Early Majority, Late Majority and Laggards). While most entrepreneurs believe the earlier, the better, that isn't always the case.

Innovators (the first 2.5% of adopters) can require much more convincing than laggards who buy because everyone else already has. In the 20th century, it could take a product decades to move through the entire cycle. More recently, these cycles are compressed and thus they have become more gaugeable. For example, did you get a Facebook account before your friends? Before your parents? Before your Grandparents?

It is much easier to get product adoption by the innovators and early adopters as they are more open minded and willing to take a risk on a new product. The most difficult step is getting the early majority to adopt the product. This is key because the majority has the population numbers to really boost revenue and transform a

---

[32]E.M. Rogers. (2003). Diffusion of Innovations 5th ed. New York, NY: Free Press.

company from mediocre to successful. Electric cars have been around since the late 1990s, but they have only recently caught on with the masses. In the early years only those interested in saving the planet were willing to purchase electric cars, but now it has finally reached the early majority and consumers believe that the electric car will bring value to their lives.

Consumers believe that the electric car will bring value to their lives. In Geoffrey Moore's iconic book on innovation, *Crossing the Chasm*[33], Moore discusses strategies to gain adoption by the early majority. These include:

- **Piggybacking:** When you buy a new computer, there is often a 60 day trial of an antivirus program already installed. Without piggybacking on the manufacturers existing distribution, the anti-virus program would have to rely on you to take the initiative to buy their product.
- **Placement:** Viagra was originally intended to be a heart medication, then later branded as a sex enhancing medication that led to increasing sales.
- **Publicity:** When Virgin Mobile launched in Canada, Richard Branson arrived in downtown Toronto in a convoy of Hummers and beautiful models named the "Mobile Revolutionaries" who spread the "word of mobile freedom".

When Greg Bay pitched *Coretection*[34] to investors, his original target market was injured athletes. However, investors thought that target market was too small to make a sizable profit. Fortunately for Greg Bay, he was able to partner with an established sporting apparel business, *Under Armour*.

With the Under Armour partnership, the target market for Coretection becomes all athletes and Greg's product can now

---

[33]Geoffrey Moore. (1991). Crossing the Chasm. Cambridge: Harvard Business.
[34]www.coretection.com

be promoted as a way to help prevent injuries, and enhance performance. As a result, Greg can now piggyback on Under Armour's already existing distribution channels. Greg doesn't have to go to retail store managers convincing them to carry his product.

While having a group of early adopters buying your product is great, the real money is made by getting your product popular with the majority. To get to the majority you need to execute a reasonable strategic marketing plan targeted at a specific demographic. Just because you build it, doesn't mean they'll come, you need to invite them.

Examples in Action

Did you know that the Startup Friendster predated Facebook as the first widely adopted social network? Despite their innovativeness, the founders were too early. The market for social networks in 2002 was not yet developed. Only innovators (that first 2.5% of users who buy first) were interested and that segment wasn't large enough to facilitate growth. A few years later, Facebook took advantage of the market's move to early adopters by focusing initially on students.

Why it matters?

Each stage in Rogers's model requires a different strategy. Entrepreneurs must be mindful to match their strategy (and budget) to the appropriate stage. Further, in order to be timely the market must be ready for your solution. Nothing is more frustrating than being too early for the market.

If your innovation is too ahead of the market, you may find it difficult to attract enough customers to justify your opportunity's existence. You may even run out of capital before the market warms to your solution. If your solution is too far behind the market, you may find your customers buying alternatives instead of your innovation.

The innovations that led to the electric car have been around since as early as 1895, but it took more than a century for the market to be ready for mass adoption.

Questions to Ask

What stage is your market in? Who were you first customers? How do they compare to your current customers?

How to Score

Give this element a:

- -10 if ...the market is at the laggard stage.
- -5 if ...the market is in the late majority stage.
- 0 if ...the market is at the innovators stage.
- 5 if ...the market is in the early adopter stage.
- 10 if ...the market is just entering the early majority stage.

© Sean Evan Wise

Element 24: Industry CAGR

What is it?

CAGR is an investment acronym which stands for **Compound Annual Growth Rate**[z] and represents the year-over-year historical growth of an industry. The larger the CAGR of a market, the faster that market is growing.

Typically, a hot market is one with a CAGR > 25%.

Why it matters?

The aphorism: a rising tide lifts all boats is fitting to CAGR—an industry-wide growth benefits all those within that industry. As a result, opportunities in hot domains (those with large CAGR) are more attractive to both investors and entrepreneurs.

The business of innovation is difficult enough in any market, so why focus on addressing a market that isn't growing? Put another way, would you rather a start a business in email security or in horse saddles? Email is a booming industry, horses are not.

While it is possible to calculate CAGR for an industry and it is also possible to access a list of such calculations, neither is strictly necessary to evaluate this element. Most investors (and other opportunity evaluators) simply go with their gut instinct when it comes to assessing CAGR's impact on an opportunity.

Examples in Action

Email, iPad™ apps, gene theory, 3D printing are all experiencing huge industry wide growth in the early part 21st Century, each of those

---

[35]www.investopedia.com/video/play/compound-annual-growth-rate#axzz1Y75xmDef

industries would be expected to have extreme CAGR. Conversely, couriers, record stores and typewriters are all experiencing contraction of their demand, and thus those industries would have low CAGR.

Questions to Ask

What industry do you fit within? What major developments occurred this year in that industry?

How to Score

The better the CAGR: the better the score. The faster an opportunity's industry is growing, the better the score. The hotter the market: the better the score. Here's a starting point to score this element:

- -10 if ...the Startup's industry is not growing, or worse yet is contracting.
- -5 if ...the CAGR is small.
- 0 if ...market growth rate is unknown.
- 5 if ...the CAGR is large and approaching 25%.
- 10 if ...the CAGR is greater than 25% and market is red hot.

Element 25: Distribution Strength

What is it?

A great solution can't be adopted rapidly unless it can garner wide distribution. That's the real power of the Internet and digital Startups. They have solutions that can be globally distributed for low cost.

Why it matters?

Most solutions are only needed by some subset of the population. The smaller the subset of users, the wider a Startup's distribution must be to garner enough sales to be sustainable.

Examples in Action

Apple launched iTunes (a system to sell and distribute music) in January 2001. Ten years later iTunes represents more than 80% of the entire digital market for music[36]. With such a large share of the market, Apple would be seen as having powerful distribution strength (i.e., + 10).

Questions to Ask?

How do people acquire your solution? How many have access to that outlet?

---

[36]www.cnet.com

How to Score this Element

Amazon's kindle and Apple's iPod are unique distribution platforms but they would only score a 5 since not all booklovers and media enjoyers own either—let alone both. Software available for direct download on the Internet is generally deemed to be a 10.

- -10 if ...the solution can only be sold onsite, customers have to come to you physically.
- -5 if ...at best, the solution could be sold nationally.
- 0 if ...the solution can be made available globally.
- 5 if ...the solution is already available locally.
- 10 if ...the solution is already globally available and for sale.

Element 26: Current Competition

What is it?

Every opportunity has competition. Your future customers always have a choice regarding how they choose to solve their problems and address their unmet needs. Competition comes in many forms: Direct, Indirect, Alternatives and Status Quo. In fact, anything your future customers choose to do, excluding buying your solution, is competition.

Let's take an example that occurs daily in homes across the United States. Let's say your teenage daughter comes home and proclaims: "I NEED a new pair of Nike Soccer Shoes." What alternatives do you, the buyer, have?

- **Direct:** those companies selling the exact same solution/ product/service. In this case, a pair of high end soccer shoes from Reebok.
- **Indirect:** those companies selling to the same customers a slightly different solution. In this case, a pair of knockoff soccer shoes. Half the price.
- **Alternative:** different solutions your future customers can buy instead of yours. Instead of buying soccer shoes for your daughter, she could wear her older cousins soccer shoes. This would meet her needs, but not lead to a sale for Nike.
- **Status Quo:** the "do nothing" option. Perhaps, your daughter should simply wear the pair of athletic shoes you bought her last year?

It is worth noting that while Status Quo is often the most forgotten source of competition, it is also the most impactful. I've personally seen hundreds of businesses fail because the "do nothing" option was good enough for their potential customers. Never underestimate the power of status quo.

Why it matters?

If your customers have more choice, your product needs to have a more compelling value proposition (see Element 16: The 10x Rule) to attract adopters.

Competition isn't necessarily a bad thing. In fact, competition can help validate the opportunity, educate early adopters and help define and differentiate your opportunity's value proposition.

NOTE: Never, ever say your opportunity has no competition. If you do, you will leave investors (and other opportunity evaluators) thinking one of two possibilities: (1) you don't know how to undertake competitive analysis, or worse, you don't know how to use Google to find your competition; or (2) the opportunity you think you have is actually such a dead end that no one else on the planet would bother pursuing it.

Another benefit of competition is that it can provide a baseline against which your Startup can be measured, illustrating the need for your venture. When your competitors do a poor job of meeting customer needs, we classify them as **Good Competition** (good because they make you look GOOD). If your competitors outshine your business we refer to them as **Bad Competition** (bad because they undermine your sales). Ideally, you want good completion as such will only drive more customers your way.

Examples in Action

Couriers are bad competition for the postal service in that they show the weakness of the postal offerings (e.g., no same day service). Inversely, the postal service is good competition for the couriers like FedEx and UPS in that they illustrate the value proposition being offered (i.e., same day service). Whether your competition is good or bad is a matter of relative perspective.

Note: There is no amount of ideal competition. Too little competition may undermine investor confidence. Too much competition may scare investors. Founders are cautioned about entering a so called "hot market". A hot market would be one that general population is discussing in the media. Ideally novel game changing opportunities are ahead of such mass awareness. Further, Companies that tack into a hot market business of others based on the hype those companies are generating are called "ME too plays" and aren't often seen as novel. Dr. Jym Morton, who teaches Opportunity Evaluation, is fond of saying: "Don't jump on a bandwagon that's standing room only". Meaning if your market is filled with tens of competitors you may need to reconsider the market.

How to Score

First, make a list of all the competition. Include direct, indirect, alternatives and status quo. Label which are good competition and which are bad competition, then use the following:

- -10 if …the entrepreneur says "we have no competition".
- -5 if …the only competition is bad. The market is filled with leading large companies.
- 0 if …there is a good mix of bad and good competition.
- 5 if …there is competition, but only from other Startups looking to address the market.
- 10 if …there is lots of good competition. Current customers confirm they are in desperate need of a new solution to address their unmet needs.

Element 27: Future Competition

What is it?

Most innovative Startups attempt to use new solutions to solve old unmet problems. But an unmet need, especially a large and lucrative one, attracts lots of companies. As a result, competitive analysis must also include a look at future competition.

Future competition can lead to what Thomas McKnight calls Ambush Exposure . McKnight defines Ambush Exposure as the possibility that some invisible "competitor" with extraordinary means and resources could find your product or service so compelling or threatening that they plunge into your market and help themselves to your customers.

Most Startups seek disruptive innovations. **Disruptive innovation**, a term of art coined by Clayton Christensen[38], describes a process by which a product or service takes root initially in simple applications at the bottom of a market and then relentlessly moves 'up market', eventually displacing established competitors. According to Christensen:

> An innovation that is disruptive allows a whole new population of consumer's access to a product or service that was historically only accessible to consumers with a lot of money or a lot of skill. Disruptive innovations, when monetized fully, can be pure gold. Amazon, eBay, Facebook, Google all made their fortunes through disruptive innovation.

Disruptive innovations, when monetized fully, can be pure gold. Amazon, eBay, Facebook, Google all made their fortunes through disruptive innovation.

---

[38]www.claytonchristensen.com/disruptive_innovation.html

- e.g., eBay disrupts garage sales.
- e.g., Amazon disrupts brick and mortar bookstores.

But in creating a disruptive innovation, and in showing the large amounts of wealth it can create, you alert the larger companies in your ecosystem to the opportunity. The best example I can think of is how offline bookstores (i.e., Borders, Barnes & Noble, and Indigo) only launched their own online bookstores after Amazon showed them what would happened if they didn't. Amazon was "ambushed" by these brick and mortar retailers who initially resisted the online world for fear of cannibalization of offline sales.

Why it matters?

Most opportunities need to be durable (see Element 15: Durability). They need to last at least long enough (and generate enough money) to justify the expense of bringing the solution to market. In most cases, the greatest threat may not come from current competition but from an ambush.

Examples in Action

In 2002, I was pitched a solution which aggregated and indexed academic publications. For years, university scholars needed to check hard copy indexes and a slew of aggregators to have a complete research history picture. The founders believed this was a huge unmet need and felt they could monetize the need by selling subscription services to universities worldwide.

Despite the fact that the founders had great insight into the opportunity, I was nagged by the Google factor. I worried if Google, which specializes in indexing and searching large stores of data, could get into this space. The concern was justifiable, I didn't think these founders could compete head to head with the search giant, even though Google wasn't even in the market yet. In November 2004, Google launched Google Scholar. This offered free and global access to academic articles and leveraged the advanced search methods and technologies of Google.

Questions to Ask?

Who else could easily move into your market? What would be the biggest future threat to the viability of the opportunity? In a worst case scenario, which **800 Lbs. Gorilla** might move into your market?

How to Score

- -10 if ...there are lots of 800-pound gorillas eyeing the market, poised to ambush your opportunity.
- -5 if ...no big player has entered the market, but several could.
- 0 if ...the risk of ambush exposure is neutral.
- 5 if ...at the moment, the risk of ambush exposure seems small.
- 10 if ...the opportunity has proprietary aspects (e.g., IP) that would make larger companies want to buy the Startup instead of competing with it.

Raising the Score

An investor once told Lipstixx, "You know if you look up in the dictionary the most competitive business from hell, it's the cosmetics industry. They'll blow your car up in the driveway." Instead of Lipstixx trying to enter the cosmetics industry it may be best for them to license or sell their technology to one of the competitors. That way, they can get a decent payday and not risk being in a fierce industry.

Element 28: Barriers to Entry

What is it?

By definition, a **Barrier to Entry** is any continuous hindrance that deters a competitor from entering your market. If the federal government requires your Startup to be licensed, that is a barrier to entry. If your Startup has the only supply of a key asset (see Element 19)) needed to generate the desired solution, that is a barrier to entry. If you own the proprietary technology (see Element 18) and are the only company able to leverage such, the IP becomes a barrier to entry.

According scholar Harold Demsetz[39], other potential Barriers to Entry, may include:

- Market Regulations
- Exclusive distribution agreements
- Inelastic Demand
- Predatory Pricing
- Sunk and Switching Costs

Every venture needs to create obstacles that make it difficult for a competitor to enter your market. The most common barrier to entry is a patent. A patent gives the inventor exclusive rights to use a specific technology for a specific amount of time, often 20 years. When Larry Brun pitched the Attitube[40], he took time to explain the unique features of his product and then answered one of the most important questions: "Do you have a patent?" Fortunately for Brun, he did have a patent in Canada and the US, which gave investors the secure feeling that if they invested in the product, the competition could not copy the technology.

---

[39]Harold Demsetz. (1982). "Barriers to Entry." The American Economic Review, 72(1): 47-57.
[39]www.attitube.ca

Other examples of barriers to entry can include:

- Cost Leadership. Get your product at a cheaper cost, which allows you to sell the product at a cheaper price. Walmart is really good at this.
- Customer Loyalty. Many people will only use Google as their search engine because they trust that it is the fastest and most accurate. We will see if Bing can break through this barrier.
- Control of resources. If you're making bamboo T-shirts and you have a way to control the flow of bamboo, then no competitor will be able to make bamboo shirts.

When shaping your idea, improve it to a point that it is 10x better than any alternative and protect your idea by putting up barriers to entry.

Why it matters?

The bigger the barriers to entry, the harder it will be for a future bad competitor to ambush your venture. Barriers to entry add to the cost of market entry and therefore serve to enhance incumbents. (see Element 34)

Examples in Action

The airline industry has large barriers to entry. First, federal regulations are costly to meet. Second, the costs to acquire all the equipment needed to launch an airline is extremely high. Third, airlines must reach agreements with all the airports they wish to fly to. These are just a few of the many barriers to entry which make the airline industry unattractive to many entrepreneurs and most investors.

Questions to Ask

Does your Startup have all the items (documents, licenses, assets) it needs to sell its solution immediately? If another Startup wanted to sell in the same space, what barriers to entry might hinder them?

How to Score

- -10 if ...other Startups are in the market, this venture has not overcome the barriers to entry.
- -5 if ...the Startup has not overcome all barriers to entry (for example, has not yet received approval to sell their solution.)
- 0 if ...there are no sustainable, significant barriers to entry.
- 5 if ...the barriers to entry are not significant.
- 10 if ...there are large costly barriers to entry, but the Startup being evaluated has already overcome them and is able to sell immediately.

Element 29: Exit Options

What is it?

In order to crystalize the value of the Startup, shareholders need an exit. An exit is an investment term used to define the moment that the shareholders (for example, founders, investors, employees) are able to cash out.

Most Startups typically exit in one of four ways: Acquisition, Public Offering, Buy Back or Bankruptcy.

Acquisition occurs when a larger company buys the Startup (either by acquiring all the shares of the Startup, or all the assets). A public offering occurs when a Startup lists its equity in a public market or stock exchange.

The IPO is the most famous public offering exit, but others do exist (for example, the reverse takeover). Buyback occurs when the Startup has enough free cash flow to buy back the shares of investors and founders. However, this is extremely rare as few Startups have the cash necessary, and those that do are so successful it is unlikely that any shareholders or investor would want to exit them.) By far, the most common exit is bankruptcy. Less than two in ten venture backed companies lead to a successful exit. That means more than 80% of the money invested by Angels and Venture Capital ends poorly in bankruptcy.

Every entrepreneur eventually needs money. Some want the money to launch a marketing campaign, others want to franchise their business and some need to build more product. It's clear to the entrepreneur why they need funding, but investors want to know, "How does this make me money?" It is up to the entrepreneur to effectively communicate how they can turn investor dollars into big profits.

If a funder asks, "Why do you need my money?" a bad response would be, "We need your $200,000 to grow our business." A better answer is, "Your $200,000 will enable us to fulfill a recent order of 50,000 units of our product. The profit from the order alone will total $500,000." With the first response the pitcher is just begging for money, with no plan on how to spend it. In the second they've outlined a clear plan for the investor to make a profit.

When early stage investors make an investment, they aim to make 10 to 20x their money back within five years. One way they can make money on an investment is through dividends, which is a share of the profits, but it is unlikely this will total 10x their investment. They can also profit by selling their percentage of the business at a later date, which can be done in the following ways:

- **IPO:** The business goes public, which is a very rare occurrence.
- **Merger & Acquisition:** A larger company buys the business, which is a rare occurrence.
- **Buyback Equity:** The entrepreneur buys the investor's shares back with profits, which is almost impossible to do.

A more unfortunate but common investor scenario is bankruptcy. To avoid the risk of losing their investment, investors want a clear vision of how they will make their money back.

Why it matters?

On day one, all Startups have the chance at a future exit. But some are more obvious than others. When a company has IP, market traction, a sustainable competitive differentiator in a rapidly growing market with large barriers to entry, it is setting itself up for a successful exit. If Ambush Exposure is high, and it is easier to **build rather than buy**, then 800 lbs. Gorillas will be more likely to simply create a competing system.

By locking up distributors, creating high customer-sunk costs and protecting key IP, a company can increase the probability of a successful exit.

Business is for profit. Monetizing an opportunity and crystalizing the future value are intrinsic in your Startup should be the goal of all entrepreneurs. Likewise, investors want to invest their money, watch it grow and then get it back. For most investors, your Startup must be able facilitate an exit in 4-7 years.

Questions to Ask

In a few years, after hitting your numbers, who would benefit from buying your company? Which 800 lbs. Gorilla would be smart to buy you? How have you made it better to buy your venture rather than build a competitive solution?

How to Score

- -10 if …it would be easier to simply create a competitor.
- -5 if …your Startup has a lead in the market, but it isn't sustainable.
- 0 if …there are lots of potential acquirers, but it is too early to explore.
- 5 if …your venture has IP that is a large barrier to entry.
- 10 if …your venture has already received offers of acquisition.

Element 30:
Government Regulation

What is it?

Does your venture require (and possess) government approval? Many industries are regulated by some level of government. In order to participate in that market a license may be needed. Government Regulations may require testing, evidence, or even compliance with certain standards.

Why it matters?

Government regulation can act as a barrier to entry; for example, regulation can significantly impact the cost to launch a product. In other cases, government regulations may influence how you sell and even where you can sell your solution.

Examples in Action

If you wish to open an institutional lending operation like a trust company, most countries require you meet certain standards (e.g., cash reserves), conduct business a certain way (e.g., can't loan millions to children under 18), or even comply with filing requirements (e.g., monthly transfer report). In some cases, governments can even require you to avoid selling your solution to certain groups (e.g., anti-money laundering rules).

Questions to Ask

What role does the government play in your industry? What regulations will you need to follow? How much will it cost (money, time, energy, etc.) to comply annually? Before your customers buy your solution/service/product, what approvals are needed?

How to Score

- -10 if ...your venture is years away from being able to sell its solution due to government regulations.
- -5 if ...there are strong regulations, it will take this venture 6 months or more to comply.
- 0 if ...there are not relevant government regulations.
- 5 if ...your venture is fully complaint, but regulations don't act as a barrier to entry.
- 10 if ...the space is heavily regulated, but this venture is fully compliant and able to sell immediately.

© Sean Evan Wise

Element 31: Partnership Status

What is it?

Does the Startup have partners? Do you know any of them by name? Do these partnerships materially increase either your confidence or probability of success for the Startup? If yes, then the venture is experiencing what scholars call the **Halo effect**.

The Halo Effect occurs when one entity (company, investor, person) tacitly endorses another by agreeing to work with them. Many Startups use the Halo Effect as a form of **Proof of Concept**.

As discussed earlier, Signalling Theory in economics refers to the impact one party's actions have on the perceptions of others. Under Signalling Theory, the halo effect caused by partners is seen as an endorsement. Take for example the following:

Startup WYZ is in the Search industry. They claim to have invented a way to search images (something the search industry has struggled to address). On day one, they pitch investors "the solution to image search" but the live demo fails and investors lose confidence in the opportunity. The next day, the founders of Startup WYZ announce they have entered a partnership with Google, to leverage their IP and expand the market. Regardless of how investors felt before the announcement, Google's signalling and halo will raise the level of interest in the opportunity.

Why it matters?

I've never met an entrepreneur who wasn't "in love" with her venture. That's the nature of entrepreneurship. Since all investors hear these claims from every entrepreneur (Who hasn't claimed to be the next Google? Twitter? Facebook?), opportunity evaluators must discount these claims altogether. But if you can't believe the founders (when they say this is the next big thing!), who can you rely on?

First and foremost, as we have already discussed, sales and customers are the best testament to an opportunity's potential (see Element XX: Proof of Concept). But what if sales aren't forthcoming? What if the Startup is pre-revenue? In that case, the second best proof of concept comes from Partnerships with known industry entities. Partnerships come in all shapes and sizes, but generally the ideal partnership will see the partner allocating (cash equivalent) resources to enhance the probability of venture success. Partnerships should advance the progress of the venture, but also increase the confidence you have in it. After all, if BIG COMPANY X thinks the company has value enough to partner with them, then maybe there is something there.

Examples in Action

As an opportunity evaluator, I know little about pharmaceutical R&D. But if a venture came to me with several large material partners already on board (for example, a leading hospital, a leading lab, a leading university or even a leading pharmaceutical company) I would glean confidence from such and say: Well, I don't know how to judge this industry, but those that do seem to like what your venture is doing are impressed...

How to Score

- -10 if ...competitive ventures have already partnered with key players.
- -5 if ...no partnerships are in place.
- 0 if ...the Startup has begun early talks with potential partners.
- 5 if ...the Startup has established a partnership with a large significant entity, but execution is still months away.

- 10 if …the Startup has established and has entered legally into many partnerships with large credible entities.

Note:

This element only covers true partnerships. A true partnership sees both parties contributing to the solution time, energy, bandwidth and resources. Some students mistake distribution agreements for partnerships. If you sell Microsoft® Word as a distributor, Microsoft® will call you their partner, but you would not score high on this element (since it is a really a distribution deal not a partnership). However you would score high on element #20). To score high on this element a partnership must be mutually beneficial and interdependent.

Plan

Plan refers to the go-to-market plan, not the business plan. The go to market plan includes:

- Key milestones met,
- Timelines and resource contingencies,
- How the product will attract customers,
- How the business will roll out, and
- How the business can ramp up further.

As you can see, this collection of elements deals with the HOW not the why of the venture. How will you get customers to buy? How will you get product to the market? How will you scale up? What keys mitigate your ability to grow? For these elements opportunity evaluators are best to look for answers that are reasonable, not right.

After all, it is impossible to predict the future. So instead of being correct, investors often use a different standard. **Reasonable not right**. Too many inventors try to convince others they are correct. They know it all.

Instead, innovators are advised to show the assumptions behind the plan and inform the reviewers that, based on those assumptions, this is the plan. By striving to be reasonable but not necessarily right, innovators instil confidence in investors.

These elements collectively represent only 5% of the overall WiseGuide™ score, not because these elements aren't important (they are!) but because there is so much uncertainty surrounding them.

Element 33: Costs to Launch

What is it?

Ideas cost time, money, management bandwidth and resources to get to market. The larger these costs, the more at risk, the lower the score on this element.

Why it matters?

Until an innovation is sold, there is always **Market Risk**. Until an innovation has sales traction, there is always the chance that the market will reject the innovation. As a result, entrepreneurs should try to mitigate costs to launch as soon as possible so that revenue can start coming in.

Questions to Ask

How much have you invested so far into this opportunity? What is left to do before you can try selling it? What costs have to be incurred before the opportunity can generate revenue?

How to Score

For this element, score a:

- 10 if ...it is too early to quantify cost of launch.
- -5 if ... costs to launch > sales to date
- 0 if ...costs to launch = sales to date.
- 5 if ...the solution has launched. Costs to launch are known and covered.
- 10 if ...the solution has already launched and selling. Costs to launch < Early sales.

Element 34: Plan to Scale

What is it?

According to The Startup Genome Project's recent report[41], the number one cause of Startup failure is Premature Scaling. The authors of the project estimate that 74 percent of high growth Internet Startups fail due to premature scaling.

What is **premature scaling**? The authors at the Startup Genome Project define it as "focusing on one dimension of the business and advancing it out of sync with the rest of the operation." Or, in plain English: when a Startup grows too fast, spends too much, and then finds revenue being outpaced by expenses.

Why it matters?

Entrepreneurs can fall into the this trap by overspending on customer acquisition, by confusing early adopters with a larger market segment or by shifting engineering resources out of R&D and into technical support too quickly. None of these tasks is damning alone; it is only the timing that impacts the potential for success.

Examples in Action

Mrs. D. has invented a biodegradable toilet paper that degrades 10x faster than all other toilet paper. She files her patent on her product, but before going to market to see if customers want her innovation, she decides to corner the market on her paper's key ingredient.

---

[41]http://startupgenome.cc

Doing so costs her millions of dollars but ensures she is the only one who can sell her product. A year later, she has cornered the market on the supply of highly biodegradable toilet paper. Unfortunately, Mrs. D. didn't pilot test or focus group her innovation with real customers. As a result, Mrs. D. was shocked to learn that end users don't like her product. So much so that her customers (the large distributors of toilet paper) won't carry it (they already sell cheap non-biodegradable toilet paper). Mrs. D. has prematurely scaled her business.

How to Score

For this element, score a:

- -10 if ...ARPU exceeds COCA.
- -5 if ...scaling doesn't match revenue growth.
- 0 if ...it is too early (e.g., products not ready for sale)
- 5 if ...the founders are holding off growth until sales justify such.
- 10 if ...revenue far exceeds cost of goods and cost of customer acquisition.

Element 35: Reasonable not Right

What is it?

Most opportunities are made up of potential value. However, predicting the future is impossible. That doesn't stop so many entrepreneurs from announcing that their 5 year future revenue forecast is conservative. In fact, many entrepreneurs misunderstand the motivation behind investors' interest in future results. Investors, and I reckon all opportunity evaluators, prefer reasonable to right.

Why it matters?

Since it is impossible to predict your revenue in five years, entrepreneurs should spend less time trying to prove their number is correct. Instead, founders should share the assumptions that lead to these numbers. In doing so, opportunity evaluators should look for what is reasonable and not what is right.

How to Score

For this element, score a:

- -10 if ...founders try to convince you they are correct.
- -5 if ...assumptions are simply a "best guess".
- 0 if ...projections never arise.
- 5 if ...the founders' assumptions are based on dialogue with future clients.
- 10 if ...all assumptions have been tested and confirmed by the market.

Raising the Score

To increase this element's score, include and present in your plans and pitches the assumptions underlying your revenue model (e.g., For every visitor to our website, 10% go on to buy our product). This helps reviewers to better understand why you feel the opportunity is worth pursuing. Whenever possible include third party references to validate your position.

The Art of Financial Forecasting
By John Pinsent, CA, ICD.D
Senior Partner, St. Arnaud Pinsent Steman, Chartered Accountants

---

Effective financial forecasting is an entrepreneurs' business GPS. Financial forecasting allows entrepreneurs know accurately and objectively where they are (along the route to success), where they want to get to and most importantly, allows the entrepreneur to receive helpful instructions along the way. For first time entrepreneurs, the task of creating financial statements, and the financial model that underlies them, is even more daunting. Having never walked this path before, entrepreneurs often barely know where the "on" button is, let along how to navigate to the mythical "exit" that is their final destination. The good news is that many prior travellers on the road to Startup success have walked this path before you. The bad news is, most of these same entrepreneurs have gotten lost along the way! But if you keep to the basics and stay the course of best practices, then perhaps you too can learn to navigate the highway of effective financial forecasting.

As an angel investor, your financial forecast is the third most important thing that I'll consider as I'm contemplating my investment. First and foremost, I need to like you and your team. Are you people that I can trust? Do you have the skills necessary to build a valuable enterprise? Second, I need to really like your concept. Is it unique? Can I imagine people engaging with it and is it the kind of business that I would be proud to be associated with? Can I offer more than cash? Once you've cleared these two hurdles, team and idea, then (and only then) will I turn my attention to your financial forecasts. Like team and idea, financial forecasts while varied, can quickly help me make that all important first decisions: Do I want to hear more?

Why are financial forecasts so important? The simple answer is that these key documents tell investors a TON about you and your business. By reviewing your forecasts, we will learn a lot about your market, your margins and your business mechanics. Through this careful analysis, we'll discover much of what investors need to know about how you nice founders are going to take my hard earned money and hopefully turn this great idea into a health profit for us all. But we learn more than just the numbers from your financials. We also learn the level of Business Acumen of your team. Business acumen ensures that the financials are realistic, achievable and most of all based on grounded real life experience and reasonable assumptions. You don't have to be right, but you do have to be reasonable.

Your financial forecasts also serve to set the tone for how the investment is going to be valued and what an investors' expected rate of return will be. If your forecasts are so far off the road of realism, then you've sent me a clear message that you don't understand your business, your market or your ability to capture value from both. If your financial forecasts are excessively conservative, then you run the risk of losing my interest by failing to hit my return on investment expectations. After all, no one wants to put $50,000 into a high risk venture, if the upside is only 10%.

Bill Gates often talks about how people over estimate what they will achieve in the short term and underestimate what they will realize over the long haul. I think he's absolutely right! The art of financial forecasting is finding that balance between **operational realism** and **infectious entrepreneurial optimism**.

If you want to impress me, as a potential investor, I suggest (and after 20 years as an accountant and a decade as an angel investor you should listen to me) all entrepreneurs keep the following things in mind as you develop your financial forecasts:

1. Anchor in the Present: I'm going to intensely analyze the first year or any period that the current round of financing will cover. I'll be interest in knowing how years two and three are expected to play out but will put anything beyond year 2/3 down to pure optimistic speculation. The key is anchor in the present and scale from there (e.g., we are projected $100,000 in year 1 revenue, and are pushing to double that in year 2 and again in year 3). Make sure the plan for the next year holds water!

2. Forget the Exit: Unless you've built and sold a business SEVERAL times before, I know that you don't have a clue about where this opportunity will take us. So, don't be afraid to dream big but know that the valuation for the purposes of my investment will rest on the details of the next 12 months.

3. Bottom-up, not top-down: Your financial forecasts have to be tied to your operational realities. If you are projecting sales of $2 million, then the assumptions upon which your financial forecast are build must include staffing, advertising, travel and marketing budgets that can realistically expect to deliver that level of sales activity. For instance. if each salesperson can make 10 sales calls a day, with an average sale of $10,000 and close rate of 50%, then to reach $2,000,000: you would need 200 sales. 200 sales would take 40 days of 1 salesperson, Same thing on the cost side of the financials. If you have product engineering work to be done, then the number of project hours needed to complete that

work must tie into a head count and related staffing budget that can deliver those hours. At the end of the day, you'll be held accountable for how investment dollars are spent. What your financial forecast should show investors is that your business will include an accountability framework that will ensure that your targets can be achieved within the timelines and budget dollars you are projecting. Remember, no one expects you to be right, just reasonable.

4. Ask for Directions. Founders all have different levels of financial acumen, notwithstanding all founders should ground their projections in reality. One way to do that is to ask for directions. Solicit input on your financials from those who have been there, done that. Test your assumptions with future clients, with potential suppliers, with advisors. Frankly, the more you test your assumptions and adjust according to third party feedback, the more comfortable most investors will be.

5. Plan macro and execute micro. Investors understand that it is VERY difficult to accurately predict the path that the commercialization of your product or concept will take. I need to see and understand the financial framework at a macro level. The details and assumptions below that level should give me the confidence that you've thought of all those details through and have a plan to execute at that micro level. If you win me over on the framework, I'll give you the rope to execute at the day to day level.

6. Fresh and evolved. Keep your forecasts fresh and your assumptions fluid. If your forecasts are for the current year and we're already in December, they really don't have much value to me. Prepare your forecasts so that they can roll

with your investments tranches and operational milestones as they are realized. Ensure that you can update your forecasts in real time to reflect operational realities such as not being able to fill a key management role at the exact time you thought it would be filled. Generally, the software that you use to build your forecasts will allow for dynamic updates to assumptions and key input variables. Stay current with all of the key data points. Remember, you will be expected to ground your financials in reality. So if you missed your sales target, you can't simply reforecast it retroactively to address the issue. You must instead, understand why the sales target was missed, and adjust the assumptions in the financial model instead.

In the end, as the investor I want you to paint me a financial picture that captures my imagination and my pocketbook. Show me the roadmap of the investment highway that you wish us to drive down together. If you integrate your framework into realistic details that you're prepared to be held accountable to, then investors will have the basis upon which they can comfortably move forward with. And in this turbulent economy, I want to comfortable ride, to an awesome destination, with a reliable driver (founder). Investors are not afraid of getting lost, they're just afraid to drive with founders who won't stop to ask for directions.

Element 36: Accomplished to Date

What is it?

Since the future is unpredictable, one can often benefit from looking at the recent past. As a result, all opportunity evaluators should ask: What have you accomplished to date?

Ideally, a pitcher should cover the milestones they have accomplished and the resources it took to accomplish such.

Why it matters?

As discussed above there is no way to know the future with any degree of certainly. While past activities are not solely predictive of future success, many investors look to the founder's handling of their personal investment in the venture as an indicator of how those founders might handle a future investment.

How to Score:

For this element, score a:

- -10 if ...the founders failed to hit prior milestones.
- -5 if ...the founders are unclear on prior goals.
- 0 if ...it is too early to tell.
- 5 if ...the founders' have used their resources well but have only accomplished some of their targets.
- 10 if ...the opportunity has a solid recent track record illustrating an ability to get things accomplished and meet goals.

Element 37: Plan B

What is it?

In ten years of venture investing, I have never seen a business end up where it predicted it would be. I have never seen a successful exit match up with the plans set in motion years before. Things change, and innovation things change quickly. As result, every opportunity needs a back-up plan, a Plan B. In fact, have a Plan C and Plan D as well.

Ideally your innovation, solution or service has multiple uses or multiple user types. For example, a billing software for law firms could probably also do well in accounting firms but it might also be used for non-billing purposes. Understanding all the various opportunities for monetization is key at the evaluation stage. After all, Viagra® was originally developed as a heart medication. However, it was the positive side effects that led to the drug's wide spread adoption.

Why it matters?

As discussed above there is no way to know the future with any degree of certainly. Things change. Competitors arrive. Governments repeal regulations. Key staff leave. You simply can't put all your eggs in one basket. Instead, opportunity evaluators should look not to the content or viability of Plan Bs, but to the entrepreneur's ability to formulate such in a reasonable manner.

TIP: Investors often say: don't try to boil the ocean. By this they are suggesting the innovator focus on the main opportunity and not all the options. So it is important that in any opportunity presentation (live or in a business plan) founders focus on the main opportunity; only reference secondary options when asked. If you lay out Plans A, B, C, D simultaneously you may leave opportunity evaluators with the impression you are unfocused.

Examples in Action

The best-selling drug, Viagra® was originally tested as a heart medication. Yet it is Viagra's Plan B that made it famous. (note: Viagra found an additional (Plan C) market in high-altitude mountain climbers who take it to prevent life-threatening edemas).

How to Score:

For this element, score a:

- -10 if ...the founders say they don't need a Plan B.
- -5 if ...the founders can't articulate a Plan B.
- 0 if ...plan B is mentioned, but seems unrealistic.
- 5 if ...plan B is known but still untested.
- 10 if ...proof of the viability of Plan B is provided.

Element 38: Revenue Model

What is it?

Every entrepreneur eventually needs money. Some want the money to launch a marketing campaign, others want to franchise their business and some need to build more product. It's clear to the entrepreneur why they need funding, but investors want to know, "How does this make me money?" It is up to the entrepreneur to effectively communicate how they can turn investor dollars into big profits.

If a funder asks, "Why do you need my money?" a bad response would be, "We need your $200,000 to grow our business." A better answer is, "Your $200,000 will enable us to fulfill a recent order of 50,000 units of our product. The profit from the order alone will total $500,000." With the first response the pitcher is just begging for money, with no plan on how to spend it. In the second they've outlined a clear plan for the investor to make a profit.

The term **Revenue Model** refers simply to how you plan to monetize (i.e., make money from) the innovation, product, service or solution. There is an ever-increasing number of revenue models. It is beyond the scope of the text to thoroughly explore all of these but for explanatory purpose, here are just a few:

Model	Client pays	Example
Per seat	a few for each user.	HR billing system
Per unit	A one time for each use.	Shoes
Recurring Revenue	A monthly recurring fee.	AAA emergency services
Freemium	Nothing upfront but pays for extras	Gmail

One of the advantages of having thought about various revenue models is that it allows you to set up for the Double Dip. Double dipping is the concept of building a solution once, selling it twice and making money from it three ways. Consider the example below.

Examples in action

I served as the business advisor for a hit TV show for five seasons. I was paid for this service. Then I double dipped by selling keynote addresses based on the work I did on Dragons' Den. Then I tripled dipped by turning that content into this book.

Any product that can generate revenues from multiple sources will be seen as having a higher probability of success. Double dipping can help outline a Plan B or can be used to afford the venture flexibility in pricing. Gillette® makes so much money from selling disposable razor blades they can afford to give away the razors (i.e., a freemium model).

Why it matters?

I started my career as an opportunity valuator during the 1990s (what would later be known as the dot.com bubble). Even in the Internet's "gold rush" days, it seemed unconscionable to me that entrepreneurs would be seeking capital prior to knowing how money will be made, but many had a blind faith that their online business would succeed. Even ten years later, I still run into innovators looking for millions in funding, prior to determining how the innovation will be monetized.

How to Score:

For this element, score a:

- -10 if …no model is presented.

- -5 if ...the model presented is unrealistic.
- 0 if ... too early for revenue.
- 5 if ... early sales indicate revenue model success.
- 10 if ...the revenue model has been proved with repeat sales.

Pitch

The next set of elements deal with the Pitch. These elements combined make up only approximately 5% of the WiseGuide™ score. In most meetings, entrepreneurs will lead with what is commonly referred to as an **Elevator Pitch**[42].

For entrepreneurs, a good pitch is needed no matter the task at hand. Want to raise capital? You need to pitch your plan. Want to attract top notch employees? You need to pitch your vision. Want to attract strategic partners? You need to pitch the benefits of working together. Want to increase sales? You need to pitch your solution. The ability to get your key message across in a meaningful, compelling, and concise manner is one of the entrepreneur's most necessary skill sets. It is remarkable then, that it is also one of the least honed skills.

By Pitch we refer to the presentation of the opportunity (both orally and in writing). Many investors have a long held belief around the value of an entrepreneur's pitching ability. Many investors see a causal link between "ability to pitch" and "venture success". Even more believe that founders who can't pitch are doomed. This is based on the issue of scarce resources. Without the ability to convince others of the merit of your innovation, founders wills struggle to attract investors, employees, partners and customers.

---

[42]www.youtube.com/watch?v=Tq0tan49rmc

Element 39: The Elevator Pitch

What is it?

The MIT Enterprise Forum defines an Elevator Pitch as: "A one minute description of a company designed to encourage the audience to become investors, employees, or customers." I define an Elevator Pitch as: A clear, concise, compelling combination of the pain your venture is addressing and the value proposition your business is providing.

A good elevator pitch is made up of two key components: the pain statement and the value proposition. The pain statement clearly outlines the need for the product and hopefully includes some sense of market size. The value proposition addresses what value the solution will bring. These two elements can be summarized as follows:

>   1. **The pain statement:** What problem does this solve? For example, people want to have sex longer than their bodies will allow.
>   2. **The value proposition:** How does it solve this problem? Our blue, FDA approved pill allows them to do so in a cost effective, non-embarrassing clinic

Why it matters?

Entrepreneurs who can't pitch in a compelling way may worry their financial backers. After all, if those closest to the innovation can't explain why it is needed and why it is potentially lucrative, who will?

Founders who pitch poorly are a concern to most investors. Remember, pitching isn't just for capital. Even when you go to recruit a board member (see Element 8), you are pitching. When you try to attract early sales, you are pitching. When you try to convince partners to sign on, you are pitching.

Examples in Action

Here is one of my favourite elevator pitches:

> People want to have sex but sometimes the body doesn't function adequately. Our aspirin-sized FDA approved blue pill will help our customers to have more sex without embarrassment, discomfort or a change to their daily lives.

Obviously, this is an imaginary pitch for Viagra® but it clearly demonstrates the two key components of a good pitch. It also passes all four tests of a good elevator pitch:

> 1) It is CONSISE—more than two minutes is too long;
> 2) It is CLEAR and easy to understand—no jargon allowed;
> 3) It is COMPELLING—it induces greed; and
> 4) It is IRREFUTIBLE—the statements are hard to deny.

Here is another of my favourite pitches:

> One person's trash is another person's treasure. Our online global garage sale brings together buyers and sellers from around the world. Some are looking to sell what they consider trash. Others want to buy what they consider to be treasure. All benefit from the proprietary trust platform we have created, maintained and enhanced for the last 10 years.

What is this a pitch for? EBay of course. Elevator Pitching is so important, we should pause for a moment to allow you to explore the process of creating an elevator pitch yourself.

In the above example, four key elements are used to sell the idea to an investor:

- **Irrefutable:** It's pretty safe to say there are plenty of people whose appetite for sex is greater than their bodies can allow. Since it's clinically proven and FDA approved, it's difficult to show that the product is not safe and effective.
- **Easily understandable:** The pitch is kept simple, avoiding complex business or scientific terms.
- **Succinct:** The pitch is kept short. Most people will give you a small amount of their attention before they tune out. Investors hear hundreds of pitches, make the most of their time.
- **Greed inducing:** The thought of joining this business should make any investor feel like they will make lots of money. The moment an investor can see and feel the greed, they are in.

Creating an emotional connection between your product and your audience is the best way to motivate the consumer to buy. For example, the Shamwow pitch to customers activates that annoying feeling they get when cleaning up a big spill with paper towels which will have to be replaced.

Catherine Langin pitched investors the Miners' Lunchbox, which has been available for sale for over 50 years. She shared the rich history of their product, and the inventor Leo May, which brought a feeling of nostalgia. After she confirmed they have made money in the past, one investor proclaimed "I love the story but I love to hear that you made money". Catherine then explained, "Leo May has sold over 1 million lunch boxes". As soon as she said that, she impressed the funders, they felt the greed and understood it was a product that could make them money.

Next time you're watching Shark Tank and a commercial comes on, try to guess the feeling the commercial is trying to activate. Try to understand the problem they're solving and the solution they're providing, and notice the key elements in them. If you can do that, you're well on your way to creating your own great pitch.

Try to write elevator pitches for the following products. Make sure they:

- meet the 4 key criteria listed above,
- lead with a pain statement, and
- close with the value proposition.

Elevator Pitch Exercise:

Pitch Wikipedia™ in only the space below:

_____

_____

_____

_____

_____

_____

_____

Pitch Condoms in the space below:

_____

_____

_____

_____

_____

_____

_____

How to Score:

For this element, score a:

- 10 if ...the Elevator Pitch undermined the opportunity.
- -5 if ...no pitch was included.
- 0 if ...the Elevator Pitch needs work.
- 5 if ...the Pitch meets all four criteria (concise, clear, compelling, irrefutable) but delivery needs work.
- 10 if ...the Pitch meets all four criteria (concise, clear, compelling, irrefutable) and delivered well.

Element 40: Q&A

What is it?

While most pitches (internal or external) usually begin with the Elevator Pitch, they almost always end with questions being asked. In my experience, it is more than just the answers being given that opportunity evaluators should review. Reviewers should also watch how the answers are delivered.

Has the presenter thought through the question or has he or she simply given a canned answer? Do the entrepreneurs get frustrated? Do all team members presenting get involved? Do all founders give the same answers? If an investor asks a question and disagrees with the answer, how does the entrepreneur react?

Why it matters?

As discussed in the section on coaching and mentorship (see Element 3) backing an idea is a dynamic process. One in which many mistakes will made. How an entrepreneur interacts during Q&A can often shed a light inside the founders' business approach. Some entrepreneurs see questions as a way of exploring deeper topics of interest, a way to identify topics that the audience wishes to learn more about. Other entrepreneurs see questions as an attack on the opportunity. The former is ideal, the latter, not so much.

How to Score:

For this element, score a:

- 10 if …questions from the audience were poorly addressed.
- -5 if …the entrepreneurs contradict themselves during Q&A.
- 0 if …there were no questions asked.

- 5 if ...most questions were handled in an open, positive and direct matter.
- 10 if ...all questions were handled in an open, positive and direct matter.

Raising the Score

To increase this element's score, prepare a list of commonly asked questions a reasonable reviewer might ask (see Appendix E) during a pitch. Once you have this list, write out short answers to each. Make sure all those participating in the presentation review both the potential questions and the pre-created answers.

Reviewers may stray from your prepared questions, but following process is sure to give your responses (and score) a boost.

Proposal

The Proposal is worth only 5% of your total tally and this is because this is the easiest element to adjust. A proposal in an investment setting (like Shark Tank or Dragons' Den) consists of at least two elements: **the ask** and the offer. But I'd argue that the best proposals contain two extra elements: the use and the results.

On TV you will often hear some variation of the following:

- Hi, I'm Mrs. Smith from Smith Falls. We are seeking $100,000 for 20% equity in our business. I'd suggest a better proposal would also include: (a) what the money is to be used for; and (b) what results will it hopefully drive. Going back to Mrs. Smith, a better pitch would be:

- Hi, I'm Mrs. Smith from Smith Falls. We are seeking $100,000 for 20% equity in our business. We are going to use these funds to add two new salespersons next quarter. With these new resources, we will triple our revenues from last year and end up with more than $1,500,000 in gross sales this year.

While it is impossible to predict the future, opportunity evaluators want to gauge the Business Acumen of entrepreneurs pitching by seeing if they have concrete uses for the capital requested and can justify the proposal with potential results.

How much to Ask for?

Even how much you ask for (in funding) impacts how investors see you. Ask for too little money and some investors will question whether the money will have any real impact on the business or, worse yet, if the company even needs the money at all. Ask for too much money and you risk overpricing your company.

So how much should you ask for? I recommend this staged approach.

1. Determine your next major milestone. This might be expanding into the US, moving to a bigger factory or importing inventory from Asia. Ask yourself: What is the next big step and how much will it cost to make it happen?

2. Then see if you can get to your next milestone with less money. The more you ask for, the more equity you will probably have to give up.

3. Once you have the revised figure, turn your mind to your company's last year of sales. While not always true, Dragons often use this figure, known as the 12 month trailing revenue, as a starting point for valuation.

4. Ensure you aren't asking for more money than you have in sales; otherwise, you may have to offer up half of your company.

I recommend pitchers ask for just enough money to last 6-18 months or until you hit your next milestone. In the end it's about getting enough money to get to a point where Return on Investment becomes possible.

Element 41: Stage & Return Potential Matches Request

What is it?

Can the resources requested be justified? Does the level of risk match the timing of the venture? Is the risk justified by the potential returns?

From a stage perspective, I have heard many Angel investors deploy the following rule of thumb for consumer software applications:

- 0-1000 users   invest $25,000
- 10,000 users   invest $150,000
- 100,000 users   invest $500,000
- 1,000,000 users   invest $1,500,000
- 5,000,000 users   invest $2,500,000
- 10,000,000 users   invest $5,000,000

From a return perspective, Returns (also known as ROI, return on investment, and money on exit) refer to how much money the investors reap upon a successful exit from the investments.

Most exits occur when the Startup is sold to a bigger company (e.g., when Google buys your company) or when the company goes public on the stock exchange (e.g., you launch a successful IPO on the TSX) and, in rare cases, when the company is generating so much cash flow that it makes sense to pay out the investor. The question then becomes, how much should a Dragon get? Does an investor need 10x the money they invested? 20x the money they invested? How big do the returns have to be to attract investor interest?

Most investors are looking to make enough returns on their wins that will make up for all their Startup investments that didn't succeed. Let's look at an example.

- If Investor #1 made 10 investments this year and all were for $150,000, then in total he has invested $1,500,000. If only 1 in 10 Startups survive to the exit stage, then that one winner must return $1,500,000 in order for Investor #1 to break even (not counting for the opportunity cost, the time value of money, and not counting a dozen or so other factors that are complicated and beyond this scope).

There is, of course, a correlation between stage of venture and needed ROI. The earlier the stage, the higher the risk. A company with early sales has less overall risk than an idea-stage venture. Further, as the level of risk rises (i.e., the earlier the stage) the higher the ROI will needed to overcome opportunity costs.

Why it matters?

Money is always needed for businesses to do any activity. Unfortunately, most of these activities cost a lot more than the business has available, which is why entrepreneurs seek capital. There are many people an entrepreneur can tap to acquire funding, but where do you start? After all, all investors aren't seeking the same kind of investments.

Most investors want to match the amount invested with the stage of the venture and with the potential returns with the risk level. Most investors want entrepreneurs to have enough funding to reach the next key milestone. Most investors would rather add additional capital after that milestone has been met than invest it all upfront.

Further, entrepreneurs who ask for more than their stage can validate are often seen as lacking Business Acumen.

How to Score:

For this element, score a:

- -10 if ...the resources being asked for exceed the level of risk.
- -5 if ...capital sought is prematurely.
- 0 if ...not applicable.
- 5 if ...the capital sought matches the need, but not the valuation.
- 10 if ...the capital sought matches the Startup stage and the valuation is reasonable.

Element 42: Enough Capital to reach next milestone

What is it?

I'm often asked how much money entrepreneurs should attempt to raise. In most investment circles the rule of thumb is:

> Determine how much it takes to get to the **next value inflection point** and add in 6 months as buffer.

An opportunity's value goes up as risk goes down. Common value inflection points include:

- Selling first customers
- Launching a product
- Filing for patent
- Scaling up to address another market

Value inflection points are milestones that increase the value of the opportunity by mitigating risk. These eventually can be seen as baby steps on the road to success.

Examples in Action

Katrina Mijares pitched Toddlerobics, and was asked by investors why she needed the money. Her response was, "It will cover the market research and advertising development" in order to establish her product as a brand. This didn't please investors, who responded: "You haven't come to the table with a process to establish that brand. I hear no steps, there's no branding."

Compare that to the response Trevor Bielby of Schmotoboard[43] gave those same investors when asked why he needed the money. Bielby's response was, "to build up inventory, to put 100 of these on the floor. I have stores in Calgary willing to sell them. I plan to outsource, but with friends we can make 100 a week." Trevor had all the right answers in his pitch and gave investors the confidence that he could turn their money into more money.

When seeking investors you have to provide them with a clear vision of how they will make large profits from investing in you.

Questions to Ask

What was your last big milestone hit? What is your next milestone? What will it meant to get there? Other than capital, what other factors will impact how long it takes?

How to Score

For this element, score a:

- -10 if ...the capital requested will not be sufficient to get to the next value inflection point.
- -5 if ...capital sought is premature.
- 0 if ...not applicable.
- 5 if ...the capital sought is much larger than needed.
- 10 if ...the capital sought will get the opportunity to the next milestone.

---

[43]www.youtube.com/watch?v=FjvBoVPSS4U

Element 43: Realistic Valuation

What is it?

A private company can be valued on many different levels and through many different methods (for example, cash flow, investment to date, value of assets minus liabilities, future potential) but in the end it is entirely subjective. Investors often evaluate a number of key factors to decide at what price a deal makes sense to them. Valuation is also about how much equity you are willing to give up, what results the investment may garner and the future potential returns the investment might generate.

So, "How do investors decide what a company is worth?" To be blunt, they make it up. Based on the money invested to date, the potential returns, the risk associated with the business, and their decades of experience, the investors may make an offer.

The true value of the company is only known and set when both the investor and the investee come to an agreement on the number. Amongst other things, a deal sets the price (based on the terms of the deal) but until you have a deal with external parties, no value can be truly relied upon, especially values proposed by the founders.

Why it matters?

Valuation (at what price are investors buying in at?) is a highly subjective element at this end of the corporate spectrum. While public companies have well established methodology's for determining venture valuation, new ideas have no such frameworks. During the dot.com boom (1997-2000), page views (how many times a user goes to your website) was seen as indicator of potential value. During the Web 2.0 boom (2003-2007), number of registered users became the metric of choice. In 2011, post-debt crisis, I'm not sure what will be used, but it seems revenue and EBITA (e.g., sales and profits) are making a comeback.

To further complicate matters, a decade ago, $5,000,000+ was necessary to get a product to market. In 2010, that number dropped to $50,000. With such a low capital requirement, many investors have shrugged off setting valuations and instead they have attempted to simplify the process by offering standard terms (for example, an incubator of seed stage software ventures, might agree to invest $25,000 in return for 5%) not based on a particular Startup, but based on a portfolio averaging approach (for example, your Startup may be worth more, but since investors can't prove that, they turn to standards terms).

Examples in Action

An entrepreneur pitched the Pizza Pak[44], a plastic pizza case that would replace cardboard boxes, to a group of investors which included International Pizza Magnate Jim Treliving (Chair of Boston Pizza). The pitcher valuated his company at $1 Million, yet he has not sold a single Pizza Pak. The founder claimed that his product would revolutionize the pizza industry without any factual proof of sales or customer testimonials. Even after Jim shared his expert opinion that his product would not work, the entrepreneur persisted with this idea anyway. The inflated valuation, the unsupported claims and the wilful blindness that he knew the pizza industry better than Jim, only lowered his level of credibility.

Questions to Ask

In return for the capital you seek, what percentage will your offer me? What do you base this valuation on (Calculated using the % and the cash being invested)? What proof can you provide that this valuation is reasonable if not right?

---

[44]www.youtube.com/watch?v=2G6edX-xQG4

How to Score

If the valuation offered is reasonable based on stage and risk levels, then score this element a 10. The farther away the entrepreneurs are from a realistic valuation, the lower this element will be scored.

TIP: In venture capital, valuation is set by the investors. So why ask the founder what they think it is worth? Mostly, this is as a knee-jerk test to detect if the founders have reasonable expectations. Many investors, won't even begin to explore an investment, if they feel the valuation is simply too unrealistic.

Element 44: Investor Fit

What is it?

While cash is fungible, investors are not. Some investors bring more than just cash to the table. Some can also add value through their experiences, network or skill. In these cases we call that investor **Smart Money**.

Why it matters?

Taking an innovation to market is a road fraught with obstacles, challenges and hurdles. An investor who has: been there, done that can add much more than simple cash. That's why entrepreneurs should actively seek smart money whenever possible. Likewise, most investors are most comfortable funding innovations in domains they are familiar with.

Examples in Action

Jim Treliving is smart money in both the food domain and the franchise business. As a result, an investment from Jim yields more than simple capital. Entrepreneurs backed by Jim get the benefit of his decades of experience, can leverage his extensive network, and may even benefit from the **Halo Effect** Jim brings to food deals. In doing so, Jim is signalling the world, that the experts back this business.

Questions to Ask

What, other than capital, would benefit your project? What intangibles would accelerate adoption and growth?

How to Score

For this element, score a:

- -10 if ...the investor has a negative fit with this opportunity. The investor is actively against this industry.
- -5 if ...there is no fit between the investor and the opportunity. The investor has no interest in this industry.
- 0 if ...not applicable. The investor is neutral to the opportunity and industry.
- 5 if ...there is a fit between the investor and the opportunity.
- 10 if ...there is strong fit between the investor and the opportunity. Perhaps the investor has a lot of Domain Knowledge or a strong industry network. The investor would be seen as smart money.

How to Score

Most investors and R&D managers are pitched new opportunities every single day. In order to differentiate yourself, we suggest you research the audience you are pitching to. The more your opportunity matches prior investments made, the more likely your venture will likely resonant with reviewers. This in turn will lead to a better score for this element.

Part III: Pitfalls

If your Startup shows signs of these pitfalls, do not pass GO, do not collect $200, DO NOT pursue this opportunity!

Pitfall #1: Red Flags

Even after more than 10,000 pitches, there are some statements that still turn my stomach. Some of these issues show a lack of Business Acumen, others illustrate the dark side to the optimism of entrepreneurship, other statements simply make the founders look naïve. In this collection of elements, we will explore various pitfalls that can undermine an opportunity evaluator's confidence in a company.

While the following issues illustrate some potential pitfalls all reviewers should be wary of, this list is far from complete. Further, some items (e.g., Taboo) are more subjectively offensive and depend on the person undertaking the opportunity review.

Finally, it is worth noting that in the overall opportunity evaluation process, detecting any of these **red flags** (a symbol of danger dating back to the 18th Century, more recently used to refer to potential hazards[46]) is reason to halt the process.

While these red flags or pitfalls are discussed after the WiseGuide™ elements, it would best practices to actually look at this issue before beginning the formal review. In that way, these pitfalls become **gating items**. Meaning once you spot a serious enough pitfall, you may wish to halt the review.

---

[46]www.investopedia.com

Pitfall #2: Showstoppers

What is it?

Showstoppers are obstacles facing the entrepreneur. These obstacles lower the probability of success for the venture. Showstopper examples include (but aren't limited to):

- The market is wrong;
- We haven't found our customers yet;
- We don't own the solution;
- Making money isn't our primary goal;
- Large Company X (e.g., Google, Ford, AT&T) just doesn't get it; or
- We have no revenue model.

Why it matters?

Entrepreneurs need investors more than investors need entrepreneurs. The supply of seed capital to drive innovation is often dwarfed by the demand for such. As a result, the best investors have many opportunities to review. In order to facilitate screening, investors are always on the lookout for reasons to say no. Include a showstopper in your opportunity presentation and you give investors an easy out.

How to Score

The more showstoppers mentioned the bigger the pitfall.

Pitfall #3: Taboo

What is it?

Some industries are non-starters. Pornography, drugs, gambling and other illicit activities are taboo and will encounter difficulty in garnering support despite the fact that they may be lucrative. Even secondary services to these industries (e.g., digital secure payments for online casinos) can be shunned for support.

Why it matters?

Uber-investor Kevin O'Leary once commented that while he himself didn't have issues with innovations based in taboo fields, he still wouldn't support them. His reasoning was based on an inverse Halo effect. Kevin felt that if he endorsed a taboo product (through even passive investment) it might negatively impact his other investments or even his other lines of business.

How to Score

Taboo is one of the few binary elements in the WiseGuide™. An opportunity is either taboo or not). There really is very little middle ground. Conversely, a very "feel good" solution, say to save wildlife, could add weight to a pitch if your Startup represents an opportunity for investors to enhance their altruistic or philanthropic side.

Pitfall #4: No Skin in the Game

What is it?

Skin in the Game[47] is an investment term referring to what the entrepreneurs have invested to date in the opportunity. Having skin in the game signals[48] (see Signalling Theory) investors and opportunity evaluators that the founders are committed to the venture. After all, if founders don't have their money invested and at risk, why as an external investor, would I?

Why it matters?

Investors for the most part want entrepreneurs to have their capital at risk prior to new capital being invested. There are many reasons for this, including:

- Without a personal stake in the opportunity, what keeps the founder from quitting when things get tough?
- If the founder¬¬s don't believe enough in the idea to risk their money; why should investors take the risk?
- It aligns all shareholders to the same goals (profit maximization).

Investors can become nervous when an entrepreneur doesn't believe strongly enough in their opportunity to risk their own capital.

Examples in Action

It is worth noting that the quantum of capital required to form

---

[47]A. Ardichvili, R. Cardozo & S. Ray. (2003). "A theory of entrepreneurial opportunity identification and development." Journal of Business Venturing, 18(1): 105-123.
[48]A. Conti, M.C. Thursby, & F. Rothaermel. (2011). "Show Me the Right Stuff: Signals for High Tech Startups." NBER Working Paper No. 17050.

Skin in the Game is subjective and relative to each entrepreneurs. For College Entrepreneurs a few maxed out credit cards would be considered Skin in the Game. For a seasoned serial entrepreneur it would take significantly more. Rest assured, no one requires you to sell your car or mortgage your home. So long as you have as much at risk as you backers, you will be seen as having Skin in the Game.

How to Score

Skin in the game is one of only a few elements in the WiseGuide™ that is binary. If the founders have skin in the game, then there is very little reason to continue reviewing the venture.

Raising the Score

Sweat Equity is not heavily weighed by external investors. Instead they look to actual cash contributed. To raise this element's score, some founders invest their own money upfront, and then use such to pay themselves (as opposed to simply forgoing salary and living off personal monies).

© Sean Evan Wise

Pitfall #5: the No @$$hole rule

What is it?

Creating disruptive innovation is difficult. Getting it widely adopted in the marketplace is almost impossible. But no matter the product, service or solution, one thing remains true: it is hard work. Everyday innovators struggle to overcome product hurdles, economic scarcity and technological barriers. For that reason, most investors I know have adopted a no @$$hole rule.

Simply put: bringing innovation to the market is hard enough without having to deal with difficult personalities. Most investors stay close to the company for a number of years, talking weekly, if not daily, to the founders they have backed. Investors want to ensure that the only source of stress comes from external forces, not internal egos.

Why it matters?

I am not suggesting that if the entrepreneur is nice, everything will be well. I am simply sharing the idiom: Life is simply too short to fill it with friction.

How to Score

The less you want to work with the opportunity presenter the lower the score. This is highly subjective and will change therefore from reviewer to reviewer.

Pitfall #6: Red Herrings

What is it?

A **Red Herring** refers to a distraction that diverts attention from a matter of importance. In opportunity evaluation, anything that distracts from the process of scoring and due diligence is a red herring.

Examples in Action

There is no definitive list of red herrings, but over the last ten years of pitches, certain phrases have become so repugnant to me that their presence in a pitch is distracting.

Here are few of my favourites:

- "We have no competition."
- "Our financials are conservative."
- "If we get only 2% of the market…"

When entrepreneurs emote the statements above, this is how investors interpret them:

- "We have no competition" ⇨ Either you don't know how to use Google or it is a really bad idea.
- "Our financials are conservative" ⇨ How can they be? In most cases financials are pro formas (i.e., future predicting) and are not based on experience.
- "If we get only 2% of the market…" ⇨ Market adoption should never be down top down—only bottom up.

How to Score

The more Red Herrings your opportunity evaluation finds, the bigger the impact.

Pitfall #7: The Key Person Dependency

What is it?

Wherever possible, find the best talent you can hire. Often these are founders, inventors, and software coders. The term "key person" comes from the insurance industry. Insurers sell a type of policy called keyman Insurance. A "keyman," or more appropriately a "key person" is a founder that is vital not only to the innovation strategy but he or she is also critical to the delivery process.

Kevin O'Leary is famous for asking innovators: "So what happens if you get hit by a bus tomorrow? Does the business also die?" What O'Leary is really exploring it the key person dependency issue. No one wants to fund an opportunity where one person has that much power.

Why it matters?

Scalability requires the innovation to be replicable. If a key person is needed to replicate the value added to the customer each time, then the business's growth will be gated by the capacity of that key founder.

Examples in Action

An artist is the key person in an art creation business. Without the artist, there is no business. If that business sells original art (or even limited prints) then the revenue is solely dependent on the artist's capacity to produce sellable art.

The patent holder is critical to an innovator's business if future R&D is going to be pursued. That is one of the key reasons that investors don't like Startups who license in their technology.

Pitfall #8: Drinking Your Own Kool-Aid™

What is it?

An echo chamber is, by definition, a hollow space that resonates acoustics. While an echo chamber may be good for acoustics, but it is not good for innovation. In innovation circles an entrepreneur who only seeks and listens to feedback that agrees with her position is said to be living in an echo chamber. Investors also refer to founders who wilfully blind themselves to the issues at hand, as drinking their own Kool-Aid™.

Why it matters?

An innovator who only discusses the opportunity or solution with those in the inner circle fall prey to downside of drinking your own Kool-Aid™. If you only listen to those who agree with you, then it is likely you will bias your judgements. Many founders want to hide their innovation from the world, afraid it could be stolen. But truth be told, not showing your innovation, not getting exposure to review and feedback, or not accepting input from sources which disagree with you, is a recipe for disaster.

That is why so many innovators in the *Lean Startup*[49] movement push for sharing ideas early and sharing them often. If the only people who have told you your idea is awesome are related to you, you may have problem.

This is where third party validation comes back into the discussion. Every entrepreneur I've ever met believes they have a good idea. Third party evidence, be it early sales or market reports or venture

---

[49]http://theleanstartup.com

comparables, gains the confidence of investors and other gate keepers.

Worse still, by not sharing and collaborating with potential stakeholders, the innovator denies themselves a most valuable element: customer engagement.

Note: Intellectual property should always be protected. In some cases, patents can be invalidated by public disclosure.

Questions to Ask

In developing your solution, from whose input did you benefit most? What feedback was given to the first industry people you showed it to? Did that change over time? For example, have you been able to develop your innovation and reflect on input as appropriate? Or has it been consistent (everyone is telling you to go left, but you insist on going right)?

How to Score

Either founders (or internal champions) are agile and open to feedback or they are not. If they are not and if all confirming data comes from close sources (i.e., friends and family) then that should be a large red flag.

During season one of the TV show, I witnessed firsthand what I consider to the best example of this pitfall in action. A hard working entrepreneur was pitching a leather armchair that converted to an all in one exercise unit[50]. To me it sounded like a horrible idea but the entrepreneur was passionate about it. When asked why he was so enthusiastic, the founder informed the potential investors: Everyone I show this to says this is a great idea. They tell me it is a great product.

---

[50]A similar company has since arrived on the scene: http://www.easyxchair.com

When investors asked the inventor whom these people were, the inventor confessed that all feedback was direct (and only) from friends and family (not outside neutral sources). Without the unbiased view, and more importantly the understanding to seek out such an unbiased view, this founder was demonstrating the dangers of the echo changer.

Raising the Score

To increase this element's score, share your idea with those who can provide critical feedback, then incorporate such directly into your pitch. Be sure to mention where you got the information from as it will show you are open to the opinions of others and agile enough to leverage such fully.

PART IV: Tool Kit

Appendix A: Glossary

1, 2, 3

800 lbs. Gorilla	A marketing term for the largest player in a market dominated. E.g. Amazon.com is the 800 lbs Gorilla in the book industry.
the 10x Rule	In order to displace incumbents, a new solution must be exponentially better, faster, cheaper, stronger, etc. Being a little better isn't enough. E.g., email was so widely adopted because it was 10x faster than traditional postal service.

A

Arms' Length.	A term of law, referring to two parties not otherwise connected. E.g., Before agreeing to a price, the buyer requested an arm's length audit of the firm.
Arms' Length.	A retail term, Average Revenue Per User, referring to how much money each user will generate for the solution provider. E.g., on average each new user of iTunes™ buys $100 worth of music in their first year. Thus ARPU for iTunes™ would be $100.
Availability bias	Our thinking is greatly influenced by what is personally relevant, impactful and recent. We estimate the probability of an outcome based on how easy that outcome is to imagine.

B

Back channels   In business, referring to an alternative secondary and less formal communication stream. E.g., Once negotiations broke down formally, the secretaries had to resort to back channels to obtain the food order for dinner.

Barrier to Entry   An economics term referring to a cost or hindrance that must be overcome before advancement. E.g. Obtaining a Taxi License is a barrier to entry for most drivers.

Beachhead   A military term, referring to a landing area first secured before the advancement of troops. Facebook's beachhead was American universities. In its first few years only currently enrolled students at American colleges could access the service.

Break-even point   An accounting term referring to the moment in time when revenue surpasses expenses. E.g., After 6 months of great sales, the Startup was at the break-even point.

Business Acumen   Skills and experience in the development of strategy and the execution of business planning. E.g. The new CEO had run similar sized companies before. He had a lot of business acumen to share.

C

CAGR	An accounting term, Cumulative Annual Growth Rate, represents how fast an industry is growing year over year.
the Catch 22 of Entrepreneurship	An economics term referring to a cost or hindrance that must be overcome before advancement. E.g. Obtaining a Taxi License is a barrier to entry for most drivers.
CoCA	An accounting term, Cost of Client Acquisition, represents how much must be spent to attract one more customer. E.g., The website spent $1,000,000 on advertising but 100,000 new users signed up. That pegs the CoCA at $10/user.
Competition, Good	An axiom representing business rivals who make your business look good.
Competition, Bad	An axiom representing business rivals who threaten your business.
Confirmation bias	The tendency to favour external information that confirms our preconceptions and to dismiss negative feedback.
Creative Destruction	A business term referring to the process by which disruptive technologies lead to massive market change. The new idea, leads to the creative destruction of the old idea, e.g., cars disrupted the horse drawn carriage industry.

D

Disruptive innovation   A technology that radically changes the market upon entry, typically generated only when the 10x Rule is in play.

Domain knowledge   Understanding the customers and the industry in your business domain.

Double Dipping   An entrepreneurial axiom referring to an activity that generates multiple benefits and revenue streams. E.g., George Lucas double dipped when he began to produce licensed STAR WARS™ merchandise thus generating many revenue streams from the movie (at the box office, from the DVD, and from other branded merchandise).

Due Diligence   A legal term for the process by which transactional material information is confirmed. E.g., Typically before a company is acquired, due diligence will be conducted to ensure all patents are properly filed.

E

Economy of Scale   An economic theory in which a venture gains cost advantages from expanding sales. E.g., As the shoemaker sold more sandals, he was able to buy material in bulk. This economy of scale leads to cost savings which give the shoemaker the ability to lower his prices.

Elasticity of Demand	An economic theory which posits that price impacts the consumption of some products. E.g., The demand for water is inelastic since, if scarce, people will pay any price for it. The price of goldfish is elastic because demand varies with trends in pet ownership, and goldfish are not essential goods.
Elevator Pitch	An entrepreneurial axiom representing a short verbal proposal used to illustrate the key points of an opportunity.
Escalating commitment	A psychological term which denotes a decision maker's increased reinvestment of resources in a losing course of action. This bias is often caused by our desire to not accept loss. e.g., The investor wasn't prepared to write off his investment in Startup X, instead he put good money after bad as part of his escalating commitment to this deal.
Exit	An investment term referring to a point in time when investors are able to liquidate their investment and claim their profits. E.g., When Facebook eventually goes public, the exit for many will be worth millions

F, G

Gating items	A decision-making term referring to an action that must occur before continuation. E.g., the investor made the assignment of IP a gating item to funding.

Gorilla Marketing	A term for non-traditional promotional marketing that relies on time, energy and bandwidth instead of big budgets. E.g., the Startup hired a chalk artist to graffiti the sidewalk in front of its customers' offices as form of gorilla marketing.

H

Halo Effect	A marketing term for the goodwill one generates through positive association with a well-known brand or person. e.g. When Bill Gates joined the Board of Startup XY, his halo effect lead to funding as investors' confidence grew.

I

Intellectual Property	A legal term for patents, copyright and trademarks. E.g., The company had more than 100 patents as part of their strong intellectual property program.

J,K

Known & In the Know	To be known is to have name recognition in a particular industry. To be in the know is to understand that industry and who the key players are.

L,M

Magic Risk	The risk associated with product development. E.g., If it is not 10x better than all other options, the magic risk will be too large.

Management Risk	The risk associated with leadership. E.g., Having never run a Startup before, the team had lots of management risk.
Market Risk	The risk associated with market adoption. E.g., Since our product has to go on sale, we don't know what the demand will be, we have high market risk.
Minimal viable product	A psychological term which denotes a decision maker's increased reinvestment of resources in a losing course of action. This bias is often caused by our desire to not accept loss. e.g., The investor wasn't prepared to write off his investment in Startup X, instead he put good money after bad as part of his escalating commitment to this deal.

N

Next value inflection point	An investment term referring to the subsequent future milestone that will lead to an increase in the overall value of the venture. E.g., Once they began selling the app, they hit a huge valuation point since market risk was mitigated.

O

Operational Experience	Refers to founders' prior know-how with regard to the building and delivery of the solution. E.g., As the Startup was producing apps for the iPhone™, some additional operational experience in mobile software was recruited.

Opportunity Cost	The cost of the best option or alternative taken. It encompasses all the scarifies needed to be made in order to pursue a plan of action. E.g., In quitting a job to pursue an MBA, the opportunity cost includes lost wages.

P

Pain point	The problem your solution addresses. E.g., the pain point of email was slow postal service.
Personal attribution error	An internal bias that leads one to blame others for their mistakes, but where one blames one's own mistakes on circumstances.
Piggybacking	A marketing term in which a new product enters the market by leveraging an existing products brand loyalty. E.g., When I purchased a bottle of Vodka, the store gave me a sample of a new cocktail mix, effectively piggybacking my vodka purchase.
Plan B	A colloquial term for backup plan. E.g., When the business plan failed, the founders went with Plan B.
Planning fallacy	A psychological term for the tendency one has to underestimate the time or work needed to complete tasks.
Premature scaling	An entrepreneurial term, representing the risk of growing the venture before it is appropriate. Pets.com failed because they prematurely scaled. Before they even sold a dollars' worth of product, they had invested millions in inventory.

Proof of Concept	Originally a term referring to a prototype proving technical solutions feasibility. Recently, the term has become synonymous with early stage revenue proving market feasibility. E.g., Without proof of concept revenue for early adopters, the inventor was having difficulty proving anyone needed what he built.
Prospect theory	A psychological term for the decision making process where risk probabilities are known and used to influence the decision.

Q,R

Red flags	A naval term for a danger warning. E.g. The sale of the Startup failed when criminal records were found on each founder. The investor couldn't get past that red flag.
Red Herring	A commerce term for a distraction from the transaction at hand.
Revenue Model	A business term referring to the method in which a venture will generate sales, monetize assets and sustain itself.
Rogers' Diffusion of Innovations Theory	A theory that attempts to explain how, why and at what rate new solutions roll out across society.

S

Scale / Scalability	An economic term referring to the ability to ramp up sales without ramping up costs.

Serial entrepreneur	A business term for an entrepreneur that has successfully exited more than one company.
Signalling Theory	A term for the influence that one party credibly conveys to another party by its action. Similar to the Halo Effect. E.g. When Bill Gates funded Startup XY, it sent a signal to other investors.
Skin in the Game	An axiom representing what founders have at stake in the Startup.
Smart Money	A business axiom representing strategic investments. When the phone company invested in mobile Startup XY it was considered smart money.
Sub optimal solutions	A solution that does not fully meet the needs of the end users. In addressing these unmet needs, Startups can be seen as disruptive technologies.
Sweat Equity	The cash contribution made by founders. E.g. For the last year Founder Y has not received a salary. He considers the opportunity cost his sweat equity.

T

Talent Triangle	A business axiom used to explain and qualify a Startup management team.
Third party validation	Arms` length evidence of your success. e.g. Sales are the best third party validation since it mitigates market risk.

Total addressable market	The subset of all possible customers for your solution.
Traction	A form of proof of concept and third party validation, this term refers to acceptance in the market from end uses. E.g. The app Startup got traction after their app was downloaded more than 10,000 times in one day.

U,V

Valuation, Pre money	What a company is worth the moment before funding.
Valuation, Post money	What a company is worth the moment after funding, calculated as the Pre Money Valuation plus the cash invested.
Viral marketing	A form of Gorilla marketing in which , each person touched by the marketing pass it forward to at least 2 other people. e.g. The video became viral the moment people started forwarding it to all their friends.

W, X, Y, Z

Wilful Blindness	A legal term for choosing to ignore a key negative factor.

Appendix B: WiseGuide™ Template

WiseGuide™

an opportunity evaluation template

(date)   (Name here for opportunity being examined)   (your name here)

Score   0.00%

Stage 1:	Pitfall	
	Are there red flags?	yes/ no
	Are there Showstoppers?	yes/ no
	Is it Taboo?	yes/ no
	Skin in the Game?	yes/ no
	Can I work with them?	yes/ no
	Any Red Herrings to explore?	yes/ no
	Is there a key person dependancy?	yes/ no
	Is there proof of concept?	yes/ no
add your own		yes/ no
add your own		yes/ no
add your own		yes/ no
	Continue?	yes/ no

Stage 2:	Element	Raw Score (-10 to +10)	Weight	Total
People	Element 1: Working on it Full Time	0	5	0
	Element 2: Been There: Done That	0	5	0
	Element 3: Coachable	0	5	0
	Element 4: Ability to Attract Talent	0	5	0
	Element 5: Business Acumen	0	5	0
	Element 6: Domain Knowledge	0	5	0
	Element 7: Operational Experience	0	5	0
	Element 8: Board of Directors/Advisors	0	5	0
	Element 9: Social Capital	0	5	0
	Element 10: Team History/Dynamics	0	5	0
Pain	Element 11: Compelling Unmet Need	0	5	0
	Element 12: Size of the Pain	0	5	0
	Element 13: Intensity of Pain	0	5	0
	Element 14: Durability of Opportunity	0	3	0
Product	Element 15: The 10x Rule	0	3	0
	Element 16: Innovation Origin	0	3	0
	Element 17: IP status	0	3	0
	Element 18: Key Asset Access	0	3	0
	Element 19: Proof of Concept	0	3	0
	Element 20: Revenue	0	3	0
	Element 21: Strong Margins	0	3	0
	Element 22: Scalability	0	3	0
Province	Element 23: Market Stage	0	3	0
	Element 24: Industry CAGR	0	3	0
	Element 25: Distribution Strength	0	3	0
	Element 26: Current Competition	0	3	0
	Element 27: Future Competition	0	3	0
	Element 28: Barriers to Entry	0	3	0
	Element 29: Exit Options	0	3	0
	Element 30: Government Regulation	0	3	0
	Element 31: Partnership Status	0	1	0
Plan	Element 32: Time to Launch	0	1	0
	Element 33: Costs to Launch	0	1	0
	Element 34: Plan to Scale	0	1	0
	Element 35: Reasonable not Right	0	1	0
	Element 36: Accomplished to Date	0	1	0
	Element 37: Plan B	0	1	0
	Element 38: Revenue Model	0	1	0
Pitch	Element 39: The Elevator Pitch	0	1	0
	Element 40: Q&A	0	1	0
Proposal	Element 41: Stage & Returns match Request	0	1	0
	Element 42: Enough Capital to reach next milestone	0	1	0
	Element 43: Reasonable Valuation	0	1	0
	Element 44: Investor Fit	0	1	0
add your own		0	1	0
add your own		0	1	0
add your own		0		0
	TOTAL			

potential total   1340

© Sean Wise, Toronto, 2011
comments welcome: sean.wise@ryerson.ca
from: *Hot or Not: How to Know if your business idea will fly or fail*

Appendix C: Sample WiseGuide™ Case

From Wikipedia:

TiVo Inc. was incorporated on August 4, 1997 as "Teleworld, Inc." by Jim Barton and Mike Ramsay, veterans of Silicon Graphics and Time Warner's Full Service Network digital video system. Originally intending to create a home network device, they later developed the idea to record digitized video on a hard disk.

Teleworld began the first public trials of the TiVo device and service in late 1998 in the San Francisco Bay area. After exhibiting at the Consumer Electronics Show in January 1999, Mike Ramsay announced to the company that the first version of the TiVo digital video recorder would ship on March 31, 1999, despite an estimated four to five months of work remaining to complete the device. Teleworld, Inc. changed its name to TiVo Inc. on July 21, 1999.

After exhibiting at the Consumer Electronics Show in January 1999, Mike Ramsay announced to the company that the first version of the TiVo digital video recorder would ship "In Q1," (the last day of which is March 31) despite an estimated four to five months of work remaining to complete the device.

In early 2000, TiVo partnered with electronics manufacturer Thomson Multimedia (now Technicolor SA) and broadcaster British Sky Broadcasting to deliver the TiVo service in the UK market. This partnership resulted in the Thomson PVR10UK, a stand-alone receiver released in October 2000 that was based on the original reference design used in the United States by both Philips and Sony. TiVo branded products returned to the UK during 2010 under an exclusive partnership with cable television provider Virgin Media.

By 2008, 25% of TV households had DVR/Video on Demand. In 2010, a decade later, 80% of American Internet users had watched video online. By 2014, this number is forecasted to rise to 52.3 million users.

The Pitfalls:

The only relevant pitfall is the fact that DVR's may undermine the TV industry's ability to monetize contents (since DVRs effectively let the viewer fast-forward and skip the commercials). This would impact the TV production industry. However, since it is the TV providers (i.e., cable companies) who sell DVR services and equipment, this may not be enough to block adoption.

The Elements

People

The team at Teleworld is working on the product full time. The founders have worked together for more than 5 years. Jim Barton and Mike Ramsay were veterans of Silicon Graphics and Time Warner's Full Service Network digital video system. While they have not successfully exited a venture to date, they have successfully worked together to bring products to market while employed as a team at their last company. The group's founders have both Domain Knowledge and operational experience. For additional Business Acumen, they rely heavily on a board of directors and board of advisors. Both groups meet no less than twice a month, demonstrating the coachability of the team at Teleworld. Because of the strong leadership team, Teleworld has been able to attract talent by offering employee stock options.

Pain

In 1998, if you wanted to record a show for later viewing a VCR and blank tape were required. One needed some technical knowledge to record a program (i.e., how to use and/or program a VCR). Further, only one show could be taped at a time. Finally, although widely adopted, VCRs were rarely used for recording. In fact, a 1998 BBC survey confirmed that although more than 70% of households had a VCR, less than 10% had ever used the recording feature. VCR tapes also produced very poor viewing quality.

Product

Watching TV is one the top leisure activities in the western world. However, since the arrival of the Internet users want more control over what (and when) they watch. Teleworld has patented the video on demand technology, naming it DVR (digital video recorder) and trademarked the term TiVo. They have worldwide rights exclusivity for the next few decades as result.

The DVR can hold over 200 hours of content. A VCR can only hold up to 90 minutes of content before an additional tape would be required. As a result, the DVR is 10x better than the VCR when it comes to storage. Many of those surveyed have never been able to use their VCR to record content. Teleworld's initial survey information showed that 92% of the test audience found the DVR to be at least 10x easier to use than the VCR.

Teleworld is currently the only provider of DVR technology, having created it in house through R&D. As the TV cable companies seek to offer more services to their users, Teleworld is in a great position to monetize their invention. Currently their DVR's cost $25 per unit to manufacture and deliver. The TiVo product will retail for $199 and the distributing cable company will pay $100 wholesale to Teleworld. As a result, the margins are strong not just for Teleworld but for the cable companies that distribute them.

Before officially launching the product, the founders had already signed a pilot deal with the BBC. This generated early revenue and served as strong proof of concept.

Province

VCRs have created a market for content recording for over two decades. However, adoption of the recording features has not be widespread. There is only one other current competitive option for recording TV content. However, this technology is 4x as expensive as DVRs and Laser Disks can only hold 10 hours of content. Less than ten percent of what the DVR can record.

Future competitors may include other set top box manufactures, but due to the TiVo patents, it seems unlikely that others can break into the digital recording set top box market. Notwithstanding this fact, the founders can foresee a day (10-15 years in the future) where the Internet may become the means of television production. If that happens, Teleworld's DVRs may no longer be needed. However, over the next decade, the Teleworld founders believe they will be able to leverage their IP to develop a DVR for the Internet.

Plan

After initial tests, and related press coverage, public demand for the DVR accelerated. In early 2000, TiVo partnered with electronics manufacturer Thomson Multimedia (now Technicolor SA) and broadcaster British Sky Broadcasting to deliver the TiVo service in the UK market. Teleworld plans to follow this strategy globally.

Scaling adoption will require cost effective access to various global markets. The founder's hope to replicate their approach in Canada, Australia and the US, by leveraging cable operators to distribute the TiVo, Teleworld can focus on product development and leave client management to the operators.

Pitch

The elevator pitch for TiVo was given as:

> Millions of people worldwide miss their favourite shows because they can't record with their VCRs. VCRs are now two decades old and most still flash "12:00" confirming that more than 90% of VCR owners aren't able to use the record feature.

> Teleworld's TiVo set top box makes recording easy for everyone. Simply highlight the show you want to record on the onscreen menu, and hit record. TiVo does the rest. Initial testing has shown the TiVo is 10x easier than the VCR to record with by 49 of 50 users.

Massive adoption, great margins and the huge barrier to entry caused by Teleworld's patents make rapid revenue growth a reality. While it is still several years from the break-even point, Teleworld has the proof of concept and early sales to show it is about to hit its next value inflection point. The founders have properly mitigated market, magic and management risk. Assuming that these seasoned founders offered a high yield investment at a reasonable valuation, one that matched the risk/return ratio of the investors, then we would score the Proposal elements as 10s. Because of this, an investment can be justified as the money would go to expansion.

The overall score for this opportunity is 87%.

WiseGuide™

an opportunity evaluation template
Tivo™

(date)

Sean W.

Score   86.94%

Stage 1:	Pitfall		
	Are there red flags?		no
	Are there Showstoppers?		no
	Is it Taboo?		no
	Skin in the Game?		yes
	Can I work with them?		yes
	Any Red Herrings to explore?		no
	Is there a key person dependancy?		no
	Is there proof of concept?		yes
add your own			
add your own			
add your own			
	Continue?	**yes**	

Stage 2:	Element	Raw Score (-10 to +10)	Weight	Total
People	Element 1: Working on it Full Time	10	5	50
	Element 2: Been There: Done That	5	5	25
	Element 3: Coachable	10	5	50
	Element 4: Ability to Attract Talent	10	5	50
	Element 5: Business Acumen	10	5	50
	Element 6: Domain Knowledge	10	5	50
	Element 7: Operational Experience	10	5	50
	Element 8: Board of Directors/Advisors	10	5	50
	Element 9: Social Capital	5	5	25
	Element 10: Team History/Dynamics	10	5	50
Pain	Element 11: Compelling Unmet Need	10	5	50
	Element 12: Size of the Pain	10	5	50
	Element 13: Intensity of Pain	7	5	35
	Element 14: Durability of Opportunity	10	5	50
Product	Element 15: The 10x Rule	10	3	30
	Element 16: Innovation Origin	10	3	30
	Element 17: IP status	10	3	30
	Element 18: Key Asset Access	5	3	15
	Element 19: Proof of Concept	10	3	30
	Element 20: Revenue	10	3	30
	Element 21: Strong Margins	10	3	30
	Element 22: Scalability	10	3	30
Province	Element 23: Market Stage	10	3	30
	Element 24: Industry CAGR	5	3	15
	Element 25: Distribution Strength	5	3	15
	Element 26: Current Competition	0	3	0
	Element 27: Future Competition	5	3	15
	Element 28: Barriers to Entry	5	3	15
	Element 29: Exit Options	10	3	30
	Element 30: Government Regulation	10	3	30
	Element 31: Partnership Status	10	1	10
Plan	Element 32: Time to Launch	10	1	10
	Element 33: Costs to Launch	10	1	10
	Element 34: Plan to Scale	10	1	10
	Element 35: Reasonable not Right	5	1	5
	Element 36: Accomplished to Date	10	1	10
	Element 37: Plan B	10	1	10
	Element 38: Revenue Model	10	1	10
Pitch	Element 39: The Elevator Pitch	10	1	10
	Element 40: Q&A	10	1	10
Proposal	Element 41: Stage & Returns match Request	10	1	10
	Element 42: Enough Capital to reach next milestone	10	1	10
	Element 43: Reasonable Valuation	10	1	10
	Element 44: Investor Fit	0	1	0
add your own		0	1	0
add your own		0	1	0
add your own				
	TOTAL	387		1165

potential total   1340

Appendix D: Sample Questions for Startups

The following are sample questions relating to each element in the text. These, or other questions similar in nature, can be used as a starting point to investigate each opportunity.

Element 1: Working on it Full Time
↳   Who works on this full time?

Element 2: Been There Done That
↳   Who has worked on similar things?

Element 3: Coachable
↳   To whom do you go for mentorship?

Element 4: Ability to Attract Talent
↳   How can you draw the best people to your project?

Element 5: Business Acumen
↳   Do you have a good instinct for business?

Element 6: Domain Knowledge
↳   Where do you get your industry insight from?
↳   How do you know your customers care?

Element 7: Operational Experience
↳   Who has delivered similar solutions before?

Element 8: Board of Directors/Advisors
↳   Do you have boards in place?

Element 9: Social Capital
↳   Is anyone on your team an expert?

Element 10: Team History/Dynamics
↳   Have you or your team members worked together before?

Element 11: Compelling Unmet Need
↳   What problem are you solving? How do you know it is an issue that needs a resolution?

Element 12: Size of the Pain
↳   If you addressed this pain for everyone who is suffering

from it, how big would that market be?

Element 13: Intensity of Pain
↳   Without your solution, what happens?

Element 14: Durability of Opportunity
↳   How big is your window of opportunity? How long will this
       window be open?

Element 15: The 10x Rule
↳   How is this 10x better than what currently exists?

Element 16: Innovation Origin
↳   Who came up with this idea?

Element 17: IP status
↳   What is proprietary about your solution?

Element 18: Key Asset Access
↳   What materials, bandwidth or other scarce resources are
       needed to produce your solution?

Element 19: Proof of Concept
↳   Who else believes in your idea?

Element 20: Revenue
↳   How much have you sold?

Element 21: Strong Margins
↳   At what price do you want to sell your product? What does
       it cost you to make and deliver it?

Element 22: Scalability
↳   Overtime, as sales ramp up what efficiencies, how can you
       improve the revenue model and EBITA?

Element 23: Market Stage
↳   How novel is this opportunity? How far along is it in the
       product cycle?

Element 24: Industry CAGR
↳   Describe the industry recent growth.

Element 25: Distribution Strength
↳   How do end users access or purchase your solution?

Element 26: Current Competition
↳   Who offers a similar solution? Who offers an alternative

solution? What are your future customers doing today to address the pain point? What makes you think customers are willing to adopt a new solution?

Element 27: Future Competition
↳   Who could enter the market tomorrow and dominate?

Element 28: Barriers to Entry
↳   What prevents others from doing what you want to do?

Element 29: Exit Options
↳   Assuming you are able to address this market need, in a few years, who would benefit from buying you out?

Element 30: Government regulation
↳   What role do federal, state/provincial and local governments play?

Element 31: Partnership Status
↳   Who else believes? Any large companies working with you?

Element 32: Time to Launch
↳   How long until the solution can be sold in public?

Element 33: Costs to Launch
↳   How much will it cost you to get to launch and then to launch?

Element 34: Plan to Scale
↳   If all goes extremely well, how would you ramp up to generate 100x sales?

Element 35: Reasonable not Right
↳   Tell me about the assumptions that underlie your go-to-market plan and revenue model? How did your come up with these?

Element 36: Accomplished to Date
↳   Since setting out on this adventure, what milestones have you met?

Element 37: Plan B
↳   If everything went wrong with your go to market plan, what is your Plan B?

Element 38: Revenue Model
↳ How do you make money?

Element 39: The Elevator Pitch
↳ In two minutes or less, what pain do you solve and how do you solve it?

Element 40: Q&A
↳ What is the toughest question you've had to answer to date?

Element 41: Stage & Returns match Request
↳ How long until you can ramp up sales to tens of millions?
↳ What ROI can you offer me?

Element 42: Enough Capital to reach next milestone
↳ How much cash on hand do you have at this time? Where will that take you?

Element 43: Realistic Valuation?
↳ What do you think your company is worth today? On what do you base that? How much capital would you need to get to hundreds of millions in revenue? For that much capital, what are you prepared to offer me?

Element 44: Investor Fit
↳ Why do you think this is an opportunity for me, as opposed to others?

Appendix E: Index

Notes

Notes

Notes